ISBN 978-0-9575023-7-6

War Crimes and Crimes against Humanity in Sri Lanka
Chronology of Events September 2008 – January 2010

Published by:
Tamil Information Centre
Thulasi
Bridge End Close (off Clifton Road)
Kingston-upon-Thames KT2 6PZ
United Kingdom

Tel: + 44 (0)20 8546 1560
Fax: + 44 (0)20 8546 5701
E-mail: info.tic@sangu.org
Website: www.tamilinfo.org

Compilers:
Mayan Vije
Dr Suppiah Ratneswaren

War Crimes and Crimes against Humanity in Sri Lanka
Chronology of Events September 2008 – January 2010

Compiled by
Mayan Vije
Suppiah Ratneswaren

A publication of Tamil Information Centre, UK

Contents

Preface and Acknowledgement

The Sri Lankan armed conflict that devastated the lives of thousands of people for nearly three decades came to a dramatic end in May 2009. The Sri Lankan government has denied that civilians were killed during the final stages of the war. Gordon Weiss, who until the end of 2009 was the UN's spokesperson in Sri Lanka, says up to 40,000 civilians may have been killed during the final phase. The government has taken extraordinary measures within and outside Sri Lanka attempting a cover up, but new evidence has emerged on the involvement of the Sri Lankan security forces in war crimes and crimes against humanity. As the government's campaign to denigrate or threaten people exposing war crimes gathered momentum, and suspicions grew of attempts to play down the crimes within the UN itself, the Tamil community felt that evidence of events during the final stages of the war should be collected and recorded. While carrying out research, we came across a number of harrowing and heart-rending accounts from people in the Vanni and relatives living in other countries. A British resident told us about the death of 21 members of her extended family, including two of her sisters, in Sri Lankan military attacks on IDP shelters in Mullaitivu. The Tamil Information Centre hopes that this publication will encourage others to continue the recording of such events.

This chronology includes events relating to the civil war in Sri Lanka and information on human rights violations, war crimes and the situation of the internally displaced persons. It covers the period September 2008 to January 2010. Many of the incidents are given in detail to facilitate wider use of the document. Examples of this would be the statement of the UN experts on 8 May 2009 on the humanitarian crisis in Sri Lanka and the conclusions of the Permanent People's Tribunal on Sri Lanka on 16 January 2010. There may be one or more information items below a date. Each information item is followed by the source or reference in brackets. Internet Website addresses are also included. Annex 3 contains eleven maps.

The safe zones declared by the Sri Lanka government have been variously called as 'safe zone', 'safety zone', 'civilian safe zone' (CSZ) or 'no-fire zone' (NFZ). In this chronology, the term 'civilian safe zone' is used, except in quotes and source information.

The term 'Vanni' refers to the general region between Vavuniya and the Jaffna peninsula. The Vanni Electoral District includes the administrative districts of Vavuniya, Mannar and Mullaitivu, and the Jaffna Electoral District includes the administrative districts of Jaffna and Kilinochchi.

The Tamil Information Centre wishes to thank all those who encouraged us to undertake this task and assisted in the preparation of the publication.

Tamil Information Centre

Abbreviations

APPG	All Party Parliamentary Group for Tamils, UK
CAFOD	Catholic Fund for Overseas Development
CSZ	Civilian Safe Zone
ESC	Essential Services Commissioner
EU	European Union
FCO	Foreign and Commonwealth Office
GOSL	Government of Sri Lanka
HRW	Human Rights Watch
ICRC	International Committee of the Red Cross
IDP	Internally displaced persons
IV	Intravenous
JVP	Jantha Vimukthi Peramuna (People's Liberation Front)
LTTE	Liberation Tigers of Tamil Eelam
MP	Member of Parliament
MT	Metric Tonnes
NFZ	No Fire Zone
NGO	Non-governmental organization
OHCHR	Office of the UN High Commissioner for Human Rights
PTK	Puthukudyiruppu (Mullaitivu District, Sri Lanka)
RDHS	Regional Director of Health Services
RPG	Rocket-propelled grenade
SLFP	Sri Lanka Freedom Party
TAG	Tamils Against Genocide
TISL	Transparency International Sri Lanka
UK	United Kingdom
UN	United Nations
UNHCHR	United Nations High Commissioner for Human Rights
UNHCR	United Nations High Commissioner for Refugees
UNHRC	United Nations Human Rights Council
UNICEF	United Nations Children's Fund
UNITAR	UN Institute for Training and Research
UN OCHA	UN Office for the Coordination of Humanitarian Affairs
UNOPS	United Nations Office for Project Services
UNOSAT	UN Operational Satellite Assessment Programme
UNP	United National Party
US	United States
WFP	World Food Programme

Sri Lankan conflict and the civil war

The ethnic conflict in Sri Lanka affected the lives of all the people in the island and caused immense suffering to the Tamil community. The Tamil north-east region has been devastated by three decades of civil war. Despite international focus in recent years real peace has eluded the country. Within the country reconciliation efforts are superficial and vehement resistance to the promotion and protection of minority rights continues to be evident.

The causes of conflict in Sri Lanka, a country of rich cultural, ethnic and religious diversity, are many: they include discrimination against minorities by successive parliaments and governments in education, employment, use of language and economic development; failure to adopt national policies promoting unity, equality, mutual understanding and trust; failure by governments to honour agreements reached with Tamil leaders; and periodic and large-scale violence against the Tamil community since 1956. Thousands of civilians, the vast majority of them Tamils, have died, and hundreds of families have been forced to seek refuge in other parts of the island or in other countries. Successive governments implemented programmes of state-aided Sinhalese settlements in Tamil areas, accompanied by campaigns of violence, with intent to change demographic patterns, deny representation in national institutions and thereby destroy Tamil identity.

The United Nations and international NGOs have documented human rights abuses in Sri Lanka, but the lack of robust measures to arrest the situation has encouraged the Sri Lankan State. Torture by the security forces has persisted for several decades and is widespread, systematic and institutionalized, despite international condemnation. The number of disappearances in Sri Lanka is among the highest in the world. No action has been taken in more than 21,000 cases where presidential commissions have recorded the names of the security force personnel responsible for the disappearances.

Draconian legislation such as the Prevention of Terrorism Act (PTA) and Emergency Regulations (ER) give wide powers to the security forces and State officers, have the effect of removing judicial oversight and suspend the relevant provisions of normal law. These laws have been condemned by UN and human rights agencies as falling far below international standards, but calls for repeal or amendment have been ignored by Sri Lankan governments. These laws, which have almost exclusively been used against the Tamil community, encourage impunity among the security forces. Despite the end of the war in May 2009, these laws continue to be in force. Human rights defenders, journalists and even Members of Parliament have been threatened with death or other physical harm to force them into silence or abandon the cause they are pursuing. Many human rights defenders have left their homes and localities in the face of continued threats and several have fled the country. A large number human rights defenders and humanitarian workers have been killed. In many of the killings, government agencies, security forces or government-aligned paramilitaries are suspected to be involved.

The Liberation Tigers of Tamil Eelam (LTTE) committed grave violations of human rights and was proscribed as a terrorist group in many countries, including India, US, UK and the European Union. The Sri Lankan State, which has the primary responsibility for the protection of the people of the island, has played a prominent role in abuses, as recorded by international agencies. Successive Sri Lankan governments have encouraged impunity, and the security forces and State officers have been involved in extra-judicial executions, arbitrary arrest and detention, abductions for ransom, torture, sexual abuse and disappearances. In the last 30 years, the security forces have carried out a number of massacres of Tamil civilians, almost all of which remain un-investigated. The security forces have attacked or carried out aerial bombardment of populated areas in the north-east region causing large number of civilian deaths and destruction on a massive scale. Sri Lankan governments have also curtailed freedoms of expression and assembly.

UN bodies have severely criticized the Sri Lankan government and have unequivocally stated that Sri Lanka has failed in several international obligations. Many of their recommendations have not been implemented by Sri Lanka. The international community, including the UN, has been expressing concern over violations of human rights and impunity in Sri Lanka for some 30 years. The measures taken by successive Sri Lankan governments throughout this period have been cosmetic, and in most instances, aimed at deflecting the criticisms of national and international human rights agencies. The governments' attitude and refusal to take action on human rights violations have encouraged further abuses and impunity among security forces and government officers.

Peace negotiations in 1985, 1989 and 1994 ended in failure, but the 2002 ceasefire agreement between the government and the LTTE, agreed with significant input from the international community, kindled hope of an end to the conflict. Norway was nominated as facilitator and an international ceasefire monitoring team of representatives from Nordic countries   the Sri Lanka Monitoring Mission (SLMM) - was appointed. Peace talks between the Sri Lankan government and the LTTE led to the Oslo Declaration in December 2002. The Oslo Declaration was accepted as a basis for a political solution to the conflict by both parties. The parties agreed to explore a solution founded on the principle of internal self-determination in areas of historical habitation of the Tamil-speaking peoples, based on a federal structure within a united Sri Lanka. The 2003 Tokyo Conference on the Reconstruction and Development of Sri Lanka brought together 51 nations and 22 international agencies. The Tokyo Declaration emphasized the need for a political solution on the basis of the Oslo Declaration, and said that in view of the linkage between donor support and peace, the international community would monitor the peace process. The conference Co-Chairs - Japan, the US, the European Union and Norway - were appointed for the purpose. Despite these efforts negotiations failed and fighting broke out again in 2006 after the LTTE blocked water supply to some villages in Trincomalee.

Final stages of the war

The government headed by President Mahinda Rajapaksa ignored the principles of the Oslo Declaration and made clear its intention to pursue a military solution. It refused to allow international monitoring of human rights and began sustained military operations against the LTTE from May 2006. It withdrew from the ceasefire agreement on 16 January 2008, which led to the redundancy of the SLMM. In the final stages of the war, heavy weaponry was used in populated areas and the government blocked humanitarian aid to the people trapped in the combat zone. In September 2008, the government instructed UN and other humanitarian organizations working in the LTTE-controlled northern Vanni region to relocate southwards to Vavuniya by 29 September 2008. More than 300,000 civilians, including 230,000 IDPs, trapped in the region, were deprived of humanitarian assistance. At the time, food supplies provided by the World Food Programme (WFP) benefited at least 149,000 people in Mullaitivu and Kilinochchi districts. The Sri Lankan government announced a 'civilian safe zone' in February 2009, which was reduced in extent in May 2009. UN experts reported in May 2009 that shipments of food and medicine to the 'civilian safe zone' were grossly insufficient and the government delayed or denied timely shipment of life saving medicines.

As the people took refuge in the 'civilian safe zone', the Sri Lankan security forces began heavily shelling and bombing the areas. Artillery fire was directed on hospitals and schools where IDPs had taken refuge. The Sri Lankan Defence Secretary Gotabaya Rajapaksa declared that hospitals not within the government-declared 'civilian safe zone' are legitimate targets, revealing the deliberate intention of the government. Photographic evidence establishes that populated areas were deliberately targeted. Observers have said that the photographs present clear evidence of an atrocity that comes close to matching Srebrenica, Darfur and other massacres of civilians. The LTTE held the civilians as human shields and shot persons attempting to leave the area. The UN reported in April 2009 that 6,432 civilians were killed in three months since 20 January and another 13,946 were wounded. But others say that investigation, including aerial photographs, official documents, witness accounts and expert testimony, has revealed that more than 20,000 Tamil civilians, three times the official figure, were killed in the final stages of the Sri Lankan civil war, most as a result of government shelling in the 'civilian safe zone'. Gordon Weiss, the UN officer in Sri Lanka until the end of 2009, said in February 2010 that up to 40,000 civilians may have been killed in the final phase.

In May 2009, the government succeeded in defeating the LTTE. The UN High Commissioner for Human Rights called for war crime investigations against the Sri Lankan military and the LTTE. The Sri government detained 300,000 displaced Tamil civilians in appalling conditions in refugee camps and refused to grant access to relatives or humanitarian agencies, claiming that it needed to identify LTTE cadres hiding among civilians. Following heavy international pressure the government said on 1 December 2009 that it would allow freedom of movement for the IDPs. According to the UN, by the end of December 2009, nearly 156,000 IDPs had been allowed to return to their home districts, but more than 108,000 remained in the camps.

Mahinda Rajapaksa was re-elected President of Sri Lanka on 26 January 2010 for a six-year term which begins in November 2010 (Annex 1). His main opponent in the presidential election, former army commander Sarath Fonseka was arrested on 8 February 2010. The Sri Lankan Parliament was dissolved on 9 February 2010 and the United People's Freedom Alliance (UPFA) led by President Rajapaksa won the general election held on 8 April 2010 (Annex 2). The government has not disclosed any tangible plan for solving the ethnic conflict and achieving lasting peace. The Sri Lankan Tamils are apprehensive that they face further discrimination and marginalization.

The UN Secretary-General Ban Ki-moon appointed a three-member panel of experts on 22 June 2010 to advise him on accountability issues relating to violations of international human rights and humanitarian law during the final stages of the war in Sri Lanka. The panel is headed by Indonesia's Marzuki Darusman and includes Yasmin Sooka of South Africa and Steven Ratner of the US. According to the UN, the panel will examine "the modalities, applicable international standards and comparative experience with regard to accountability processes, taking into account the nature and scope of any alleged violations in Sri Lanka." The Sri Lankan government has refused to cooperate with the UN panel and President Rajapaksa has said that he did not care about the damage to the country's image as a result of resisting UN investigations.

September 2008

War Crimes and Crimes against Humanity in Sri Lanka
Chronology of Events September 2008 - January 2010

2008

8 September

The Sri Lankan government instructed UN and other humanitarian organizations working in LTTE-controlled Vanni to relocate south to Vavuniya by 29 September 2008. The NGO secretariat of the government said in a letter to humanitarian agencies: "Secretary to the Ministry of Defence, Public Security, Law and Order has advised in his letter dated 05/09/2008 and numbered SMOD/320/DEM/GEN(45), to inform all the NGOs registered in this office that no expatriate/employee or any other person employed by an NGO and working in the Vanni will be permitted to travel beyond the Omanthai checkpoint, in consideration of prevailing security situation". The letter also instructed agencies working in the Vanni to "withdraw/remove all the assets (vehicles, machinery and equipment) and all employees who are not permanent residents in Vanni, with immediate effect".

There were at least 160,000 Tamil IDPs in the districts of Mullaitivu and Kilinochchi under LTTE control, according to the UN Inter-Agency Standing Committee (IASC). Heavy fighting in the south-western parts of the Vanni forced more than 70,000 people to flee their homes in the previous two months. Food supplies provided by the World Food Programme benefited at least 149,000 people in the two districts, the IASC said.
[*SRI LANKA: UN, NGOs to pull out from north*, UN Inter-Agency Standing Committee, 10 September 2008 - www.irinnews.org/Report.aspx?ReportId=80272]

9 September

The Sri Lankan air force bombed Puthukudyiruppu in Mullaitivu District damaging several buildings including the Sri Subramaniya Vidyalayam (school), and wounding a civilian.
[*SLAF bombs school in Puthukudyiruppu town*, TamilNet, 9 September 2008 - www.tamilnet.com/art.html?catid=13&artid=26872]

Reports said that many schools in the Vanni had been abandoned, along with books, other educational materials and furniture, as school Principals, teachers and students have been displaced. The Zonal Director of Education for Kilinochchi had reported on 21 August 2008 that since June 2008, 33 schools were abandoned, as a result of 10,000 students being displaced from areas in Poonakari and Karachchi AGA divisions in Kilinochchi District. The Zonal of Director Education for Vavuniya North reported that 42 schools (which had 3,498 students) were abandoned due to shelling during June-July 2008.

Many schools are being used to accommodate displaced people and educational activities in these schools have been affected. The District Secretariat of Kilinochchi said that displaced people were sheltering in 22 government schools. UNICEF reported that educational materials had been lost due to multiple displacements and the quantity of materials was insufficient.

September 2008

[*Humanitarian Crisis in Vanni*, Christian Solidarity Movement (CSM), 9th September 2008
http://omiusajpic.org/files/2008/11/vanni-situation-csm-background-note-09sept08-2.pdf]

In a press release, the All-Party Parliamentary Group (APPG) of the British House of Commons deplored Sri Lanka's decision to bar foreign aid staff from LTTE-controlled area in the Vanni at a critical juncture when internally displaced people (IDP) most needed help of the aid staff. The APPG demanded Britain to issue a public condemnation and follow up with firm actions including UN sanctions.

[*Sri Lanka's decision to bar foreign aid staff – Britain must act now*, Press Statement, All-Party Parliamentary Group for Tamils, House of Commons, 9 September 2008 -
www.tamilsforum.com/press%20release%20-%20appg%20on%20banning%20ngos%20in%20wanni%2009092008.pdf]

10 September

Three Tamil civilians, including an 11 year-old child, were wounded and 23 houses were damaged when the Sri Lankan air force bombed Kilinochchi town.

[*SLAF bombs Kilinochchi town, 3 civilians wounded*, TamilNet, 10 September 2008 -
www.tamilnet.com/art.html?catid=13&artid=26884]

18 September

The office of the International Committee of the Red Cross (ICRC) at Iranaimadu Junction in Kilinochchi District was relocated to Ratnapuram in Kilinochchi town, after shells fired by the Sri Lanka army exploded in the vicinity of the office.

[*ICRC relocates in Kilinochchi*, TamilNet, Thursday, 18 September 2008
www.tamilnet.com/art.html?catid=13&artid=26979]

21 September

Following a government order requiring all Tamils in Colombo who had fled the five war-torn northern Sri Lankan districts in the past five years to register with the police, the process began in special registration centres. Defence Secretary Gotabaya Rajapaksa said people without a valid reason to stay should leave the capital.

[*Tamil census ordered in Colombo*, BBC, 21 September 2008
http://news.bbc.co.uk/1/hi/world/south_asia/7627821.stm]

26 September

Vijitharanjini Ravichandran, 26, suffered serious injuries in a Sri Lanka army artillery attack at Uruthirapuram in Kilinochchi District. She was admitted to Kilinochchi hospital.

[*SLA shells Kilinochchi suburb, IDP mother injured*, TamilNet, 26 September 2008 -
www.tamilnet.com/art.html?catid=13&artid=27033]

27 September

Civilian Ranganathan Sathees, 26, was killed and eight others, including four children, were wounded in a Sri Lanka air force attack at Ratnapuram, in Kilinochchi town.

[*Civilian killed, 8 including 4 children wounded in SLAF attack*, TamilNet, 27 September 2008 -
www.tamilnet.com/art.html?catid=13&artid=27042]

September 2008

28 September

Five Tamil civilians were wounded when the Sri Lanka army fired artillery shells at houses between 155 Mile Post and Iranaimadu junction in Kilinochchi District.

[*5 civilians wounded in SLA shelling in Kilinochchi*, TamilNet, 28 September 2008 - www.tamilnet.com/art.html?catid=13&artid=27053]

October 2008

1 October

Two Tamil civilians were killed and 13 others were wounded in an air force attack south of Kilinochchi town. Nineteen houses were destroyed in the attack.

[*2 civilians killed, 13 wounded in SLAF attack on Kilinochchi suburb*, 1 October 2008 www.tamilnet.com/art.html?catid=13&artid=27074]

4 October

Human Rights Minister Mahinda Samarasinghe said at a press conference that the Project Manager of Dutch agency ZOA Refugee Care, who defied the government order to all NGO staff to leave Kilinochchi, will be deported immediately. Defence Secretary Gotabaya Rajapaksa accused the Italian national of links with the LTTE.

[*ZOA project manager to be deported immediately*, The Island (Sri Lanka), October 4, 2008 www.island.lk/2008/10/04/news1.html]

10 October

Three Tamil civilians, including a child, were killed and six others were injured in Sri Lanka air force strikes in Paranthan, north of Kilinochchi town. Twelve houses were destroyed, and the Kumarapuram Murugan Hindu temple and a shop were damaged.

[*3 civilians killed in Sri Lankan air-strike, IDP teacher, daughter among victims*, TamilNet, 10 October 2008 www.tamilnet.com/art.html?catid=13&artid=27153]

28 October

Muniyandi Chandranayagam, 59, was wounded in a Sri Lanka air force attack at Kanakapuram near Kilinochchi-Akkarayan Road in Kilinochchi District.

[*Civilian killed, SLA steps up artillery barrage on Kilinochchi suburbs*, TamilNet, 30 October 2008 www.tamilnet.com/art.html?catid=13&artid=27318]

An LTTE light-wing aircraft dropped two bombs on the Kelanitissa power station, near Colombo causing minor damage to the station which handles 75% of the power distribution in the country. The aircraft caused panic in Colombo as anti-aircraft guns were fired in the high security zone housing the harbour, Presidential Office and several hotels. LTTE aircraft also dropped three bombs on Thallady military camp in Mannar District damaging the camp and injuring a soldier.

[*LTTE breaches Colombo security*, The Hindu (India), 30 October 2008 www.hinduonnet.com/2008/10/30/stories/2008103061421800.htm]

29 October

A Tamil civilian was killed at Ratnapuram suburb when the Sri Lanka army fired artillery shells on Kilinochchi town.

[*Civilian killed, SLA steps up artillery barrage on Kilinochchi suburbs*, TamilNet, 30 October 2008 - www.tamilnet.com/art.html?catid=13&artid=27318]

31 October

The Sri Lanka air force attacked the Kilinochchi suburb of Jeyanthinagar, damaging seven houses.

[*Civilian houses damaged in SLAF attack on Kilinochchi suburb*, TamilNet, Friday, 31 October 2008 ww.tamilnet.com/art.html?catid=13&artid=27346]

November 2008

6 November

Sri Lanka air force bombers attacked Paranathan, north of Kilinochchi, destroying at least five houses.
[*SLAF bombs Paranthan suburb*, TamilNet, 6 November 2008 -
www.tamilnet.com/art.html?catid=13&artid=27405]

14 & 15 November

Sri Lanka army's artillery fire on 14 and 15 November destroyed several houses in Kilinochchi town.
[*SLA continues artillery barrage on Kilinochchi town*, TamilNet, 15 November 2008,
www.tamilnet.com/art.html?catid=13&artid=27484]

17 November

The Sri Lanka army shelled Paranthan, killing M. Sathiyathevan, 24, and wounding six others. Many houses and shops were destroyed in the attack.
[*SLA artillery barrage kills civilian in Paranthan, 6 wounded*, TamilNet, 17 November 2008 -
www.tamilnet.com/art.html?catid=13&artid=27498]

27 November

Norwegian Refugee Council's (NRC) construction-supervisor A. Vigneswaran, 28, was abducted from his home by unidentified gunmen in Batticaloa and shot dead.
[*NRC Staff Member Killed in Sri Lanka*, Norwegian Refugee Council, 2 December 2008 -
www.nrc.no/?did=9357635]

29 November

Sri Lanka air force bombers attacked a refugee camp near Dharmapuram in Kilinochchi District killing three Tamil civilians. Two other persons, including a 5 year-old child, wounded in the attack, later died in the hospital. At least 18 others including seven children suffered injuries.
[*SLAF bombs refugee camp in 'secure zone' in Vanni, children among victims*,
TamilNet, 29 November 2008   www.tamilnet.com/art.html?catid=13&artid=27618]

December 2008

15 December

The Mullaitivu General Hospital was shelled by the Sri Lanka army. Two patients were injured and a ward and medical equipment were damaged.

[*Sri Lanka Repeated shelling of hospitals evidence of war crimes*, Human Rights Watch, 8 May 2009
www.hrw.org/en/news/2009/05/08/sri-lanka-repeated-shelling-hospitals-evidence-war-crimes]

17 December

Five month-old Rajithan Ravishankar and Jeyasundraram Selvaratnam, 25, were killed and 13 other internally displaced persons (IDP) including three children were wounded when Sri Lanka air force planes bombed refugee settlements in Vaddakkachchi in Kilinochchi District.

[*SLAF bombs refugee settlements: 2 killed, 13 wounded, 4 child victims*, TamilNet, 17 December 2008 -
www.tamilnet.com/art.html?catid=13&artid=27759]

19 December

The Sri Lanka army fired five shells on Mullaitivu General Hospital. Some wards, the operating theatre and the Medical Superintendent's headquarters were damaged. Two hospital staff were wounded.

[*Sri Lanka Repeated shelling of hospitals evidence of war crimes*, Human Rights Watch, 8 May 2009 -
www.hrw.org/en/news/2009/05/08/sri-lanka-repeated-shelling-hospitals-evidence-war-crimes]

20 December

The Sri Lanka army fired shells killing two civilians in Vaddakkachchi in Kilinochchi District. Several houses were damaged in the attack.

[*2 civilians killed in SLA shelling in Vaddakkachchi*, TamilNet, 20 December 2008 -
www.tamilnet.com/art.html?catid=13&artid=27794]

Shells fired by the Sri Lanka army exploded inside the grounds of Mullaitivu General Hospital.

[*Sri Lanka Repeated shelling of hospitals evidence of war crimes*, Human Rights Watch, 8 May 2009 -
www.hrw.org/en/news/2009/05/08/sri-lanka-repeated-shelling-hospitals-evidence-war-crimes]

22 December

The Sri Lanka air force bombed the area near Kilinochchi General Hospital. Shrapnel caused damages to the hospital building.

[*Sri Lanka Repeated shelling of hospitals evidence of war crimes*, Human Rights Watch, 8 May 2009
www.hrw.org/en/news/2009/05/08/sri-lanka-repeated-shelling-hospitals-evidence-war-crimes]

25 December

Three buildings of the Kilinochchi General Hospital were damaged by Sri Lanka army shells. The new-born nursing section for mothers, Outpatients Department, and the hospital reception building were damaged in the attack.

[*Sri Lanka Repeated shelling of hospitals evidence of war crimes*, Human Rights Watch, 8 May 2009 -
www.hrw.org/en/news/2009/05/08/sri-lanka-repeated-shelling-hospitals-evidence-war-crimes]

30 December

Sri Lanka army shells hit the Kilinochchi General Hospital causing damage to the building.

[*Sri Lanka Repeated shelling of hospitals evidence of war crimes*, Human Rights Watch, 8 May 2009 -
www.hrw.org/en/news/2009/05/08/sri-lanka-repeated-shelling-hospitals-evidence-war-crimes]

January 2009

2009

1 January

The Sri Lanka air force bombed Murasumoddai in Kilinochchi District, killing five Tamil civilians and injuring 28 others, including five children.

[*5 killed, 28 wounded in SLAF attacks on Murasumoddai for second day*, TamilNet, 1 January 2009 - www.tamilnet.com/art.html?catid=13&artid=27884]

2 January

Four Tamil civilians were killed and eight others were wounded when the Sri Lanka air force bombed a service station and a bus depot near Mullaitivu town. The injured were admitted to the Puthukudyiruppu hospital.

[*4 civilians killed, SLAF bombs petrol station, bus depot in Mullaitivu*, TamilNet, 2 January 2009 - www.tamilnet.com/art.html?catid=13&artid=27900]

Sri Lanka army shells killed a Tamil civilian and wounded ten people at Murasumoddai in Kilinochchi District.

[*SLA shelling kills civilian, 10 wounded in Vanni*, TamilNet, 2 January 2009 www.tamilnet.com/art.html?catid=13&artid=27899]

4 January

Thirteen Tamil civilians were injured in Sri Lanka army shell attacks in Murasumoaddai, Puliyampokkanai, Vaddakkachchi, Dharmapuram and Paranthan in Kilinochchi District. They were admitted to the Dharmapuram hospital.

[*13 civilians wounded in SLA artillery barrage*, TamilNet, 4 January 2009 - www.tamilnet.com/art.html?catid=13&artid=27916]

8 January

Sunday Leader newspaper editor Lasantha Wickrematunga, 52, was shot dead by two men on a motorcycle as he drove to work in the morning in Colombo. Mr. Wickrematunga was often the target of intimidation attempts and libel suits, including a lawsuit by the President's brother, Gotabaya Rajapaksa. Reporters Sans Frontieres (RSF) said: "President Mahinda Rajapaksa, his associates and the government media are directly to blame because they incited hatred against him and allowed an outrageous level of impunity to develop as regards violence against the press". The *Sunday Leader* was highly critical of government policy on the war with the LTTE and reported often on high-level corruption in arms procurement deals involving government ministers.

[*Outrage at fatal shooting of newspaper editor in Colombo*, Reporters Sans Frontieres, 8 January 2009 - www.rsf.org/Outrage-at-fatal-shooting-of.html]

Three Tamil civilians, including a child, were killed in Sri Lanka army shelling at Vaddakkachchi in Kilinochchi District. The nine people wounded, including three children, were admitted to Dharmapuram hospital.

[*3 civilians, including child, killed in SLA shelling in Vanni*, TamilNet, 8 January 2009 www.tamilnet.com/art.html?catid=13&artid=27948]

January 2009

Shells fired by the Sri Lanka army exploded near Dharmapuram hospital in Kilinochchi District killing seven Tamil civilians.

[*Sri Lanka Repeated shelling of hospitals evidence of war crimes*, Human Rights Watch, 8 May 2009 - www.hrw.org/en/news/2009/05/08/sri-lanka-repeated-shelling-hospitals-evidence-war-crimes]

9 January

Following significant military developments in northern Sri Lanka, the European Union Heads of Mission in Colombo called upon the Sri Lanka government and other parties to minimise the impact of the conflict on the civilian population and civil society, in particular by ensuring that humanitarian needs in the north are properly assessed and met, and by ensuring that civil society is able to operate without impediment. In particular EU Heads of Mission strongly condemned the repeated attacks on and intimidation of the media, including the armed attack on the MTV TV-station and the brutal assassination of the *Sunday Leader*'s Chief Editor, and urged the Sri Lankan authorities to take all necessary steps to bring the perpetrators to justice.

[*Statement by EU Heads of Mission in Colombo*, European Union, 09/01/2009 www.dellka.ec.europa.eu/en/whatsnew/2009/HTML/PR-HoM_090109.htm]

10 January

Four Tamil IDP civilians, including two students, were killed when the Sri Lanka army fired shells on Puthukudyiruppu in Mullaitivu District. Four other civilians, including a child, were injured.

[*4 killed, SLA artillery targets civilian settlement in Puthukkudyiruppu*, TamilNet, 11 January 2009 www.tamilnet.com/art.html?catid=13&artid=27981]

11 January

Shells fired by the Sri Lanka army destroyed the office of the Deputy Provincial Director of Health Services at Puliyampokkanai in Kilinochchi District.

[*SLA shells hit Health Secretariat of Kilinochchi district*, TamilNet, 11 January 2009 - www.tamilnet.com/art.html?catid=13&artid=27990]

13 January

The Puthukudyiruppu hospital in Mullaitivu District was hit by shells fired by the Sri Lanka army. A Tamil civilian was killed and six others were wounded. Patients fled the wards seeking shelter from the shelling.

[*Sri Lanka Repeated shelling of hospitals evidence of war crimes*, Human Rights Watch, 8 May 2009 - www.hrw.org/en/news/2009/05/08/sri-lanka-repeated-shelling-hospitals-evidence-war-crimes]

16 January

Five Tamil civilians, including two children, were killed and seven others were wounded in artillery attacks on Kaiveli, Kompavil and Viswamadu in Mullaitivu District. The wounded were admitted to Puthukudyiruppu hospital.

[*5 civilians killed, 7 injured in Sri Lankan artillery attack*, TamilNet, 16 January 2009 www.tamilnet.com/art.html?catid=13&artid=28035]

17 January

Following a discussion with Ministers, Governor of the North, Provincial Council Secretaries, Government Agents, Divisional Secretaries and security officials in Colombo, Presidential Advisor

January 2009

Basil Rajapaksa disclosed that arrangements had been made to set up refugee welfare centres in Menik Farm 1 (150 acres), Menik Farm 2 (450 acres) and Omanthai (150 acres) in Vavuniya District, to accommodate Tamil IDPs arriving from the Vavuniya, Mannar, Mullaitivu, Kilinochchi and Jaffna districts.

[*Relief welfare centres for IDPs*, Daily News (Sri Lanka), 20 January 2009
www.dailynews.lk/2009/01/20/news11.asp]

Artillery shells killed four Tamil civilians and injured 11 others at Viswamadu and Puthukudyiruppu in Mullaitivu District.

[*Sri Lankan shelling kills 4 civilians, children among 11 wounded*, TamilNet, 18 January 2009 -
www.tamilnet.com/art.html?catid=13&artid=28048]

18 January

Eighteen Tamil civilians were killed in Sri Lanka army artillery attacks at Valluvarpuram, Mayilvakanapuram, Theravil, Manikkapuram, Viswamadu, Punnaineeravi and Chundikkulam, in Kilinochchi and Mullaitivu districts. Forty two others, including many children, were wounded.

[*Vanni civilians under deadly siege*, TamilNet, 18 January 2009 –
www.tamilnet.com/art.html?catid=13&artid=28054; *Artillery barrage kills several civilians, dozens wounded within 24 hours*, TamilNet, 18 January 2009 - www.tamilnet.com/art.html?catid=13&artid=28054]

19 January

A shell fired by the Sri Lanka army fell in the yard of the Mullaitivu makeshift hospital in a school at Vallipunam. Six people in the Out-Patients Ward were injured.

[*Sri Lanka Repeated shelling of hospitals evidence of war crimes*, Human Rights Watch, 8 May 2009
www.hrw.org/en/news/2009/05/08/sri-lanka-repeated-shelling-hospitals-evidence-war-crimes]

Fifteen Tamil civilians, including 5 children, were killed and 29 others were injured in shell attacks by the Sri Lanka army on IDP settlements at Viswamadu, Udaiyarkaddu, Suthanthirapuram and Manikkapuram in Mullaitivu District.

[*Unprecedented civilian carnage in Vanni*, TamilNet, 20 January 2009 -
www.tamilnet.com/art.html?catid=13&artid=28076]

21 January

Military spokesman Brigadier Udaya Nanayakkara announced that the army headquarters had demarcated a 'civilian safe zone', around 28 sq km in extent, in Mullaitivu District. With effect from 21 January 2009, the 'civilian safe zone' is as follows: A four km long stretch to the north of Udayarkaddu junction and Yellow Bridge on the A-35 Puthukudyiruppu–Paranthan road up to Iruddumadu and another 8 km long area from the South of Iruddumadu up to Thevapuram. Both southern boundaries of Udayarkaddu junction and Yellow Bridge touch the edge of the A-35 road as the demarcated safe zone is located north of the A-35 road (Annex 3).

[*Army expands safe zone for entrapped civilians - Mullaitivu*, Ministry of Defence Sri Lanka, 22 January 2009
www.defence.lk/new.asp?fname=20090121_05]

A shell hit the Mullaitivu makeshift hospital at Vallipunam in Mullaitivu District.

January 2009

[*Sri Lanka Repeated shelling of hospitals evidence of war crimes*, Human Rights Watch, 8 May 2009
www.hrw.org/en/news/2009/05/08/sri-lanka-repeated-shelling-hospitals-evidence-war-crimes]

22 January
Many Tamil civilians were killed in Vallipunam and Thevipuram in Mullaitivu District in three days of Sri Lanka army artillery and multi-barrel rocket launcher fire. According to Mullaitivu Regional Director of Health Service, Dr. T. Varatharajah, 16 civilians were killed on 20 January, 20 on 21 January and 30 on 22 January. More than 200 people were injured.
[*66 civilians killed within 3 days - Mullai RDHS*, TamilNet, 22 January 2009,
www.tamilnet.com/art.html?catid=13&artid=28094]

The intensive care unit and the surgical area of the Mullaitivu makeshift hospital at Vallipunam were damaged in Sri Lanka army artillery fire. Five Tamil civilians were killed within the hospital premises. Twenty two people, including two hospital medical staff, were injured.
[*Sri Lanka Repeated shelling of hospitals evidence of war crimes*, Human Rights Watch, 8 May 2009 -
www.hrw.org/en/news/2009/05/08/sri-lanka-repeated-shelling-hospitals-evidence-war-crimes]

23 January
Sri Lanka army artillery shells killed five Tamil civilians, including a child, and injured 83 others at Moongilaru, Iruddumadu, Mylvaganapuram, Udaiyarkaddu, Thevipuram and Vallipunam in Kilinochchi and Mullaitivu districts. Several IDP settlements within the 'civilian safe zone' came under fire.
[*'Safety zone' shelled again, 5 civilians killed, 83 wounded*, TamilNet, 23 January 2009 -
www.tamilnet.com/art.html?catid=13&artid=28124]

24 January
Seven Tamil civilians were killed and 87 others were wounded when the Sri Lanka army shelled Udaiyarkaddu in Mullaitivu District. The hospital at Udaiyarkaddu came under attack.
[*12 civilians killed, 87 wounded, SLA continues artillery attack on 'safety zone'*, TamilNet, 24 January 2009 -
www.tamilnet.com/art.html?catid=13&artid=28133]

25 January
Shelling by the Sri Lanka army in populated areas including the 'civilian safe zone' in Suthanthirapuram, Udaiyarkaddu and Theravil in Visvamadu killed 22 Tamil civilians and injured more than 60 others. Two shells fell on a humanitarian supply centre run by the World Food Programme (WFP), killing five members of a family. Many children were among the dead and wounded.
[*SLA shelling kills 22 civilians, wounds 60, targets humanitarian supply centre*, TamilNet, 25 January 2009
www.tamilnet.com/art.html?catid=13&artid=28137]

26 January
In a letter of appeal under the heading "Human catastrophe and medical emergency in the Vanni", Mullaitivu Regional Director of Health Services Dr. T. Varatharajah said that heavy fighting and continuous multi-barrel artillery shelling had killed more than 300 IDPs and injured over 1,000 people in the 'civilian safe zone' in Mullaitivu District, including Vallipunam, Moongilaru and Udaiyarkaddu areas. He appealed to the Sri Lanka government, ICRC and the UN for medical supplies

January 2009

and medical teams, and warned that the nature of injuries and the number of injuries is such that if medicines did not arrive in the next 24 hours, many of the injured will die. Dr. Varatharajah appealed for blood bags, blood transfusion sets, intravenous (IV) fluid, antibiotics, dressings, morphine, pain killers, anaesthetic drugs and other medical supplies.

[*100 civilians feared killed, countless wounded, artillery barrage on 'safety zone'*, TamilNet, 26 January 2009 – www.tamilnet.com/art.html?catid=13&artid=28144; *More than 1,000 wounded, Mullai RDHS urges IC to send medical teams*, TamilNet, 26 January 2009   www.tamilnet.com/art.html?catid=13&artid=28153]

Ten patients were killed and 40 others were injured by Sri Lanka army shells in the makeshift hospital at Udaiyarkaddu in Mullaitivu District. Four ambulances were damaged.

[*Sri Lanka Repeated shelling of hospitals evidence of war crimes*, Human Rights Watch, 8 May 2009 - www.hrw.org/en/news/2009/05/08/sri-lanka-repeated-shelling-hospitals-evidence-war-crimes]

27 January

Norwegian Foreign Affairs Minister Jonas Gahr Støre condemned the conduct of hostilities in Sri Lanka which caused unacceptable suffering to civilians. "I am deeply concerned about the situation of the civilians who are trapped in the areas where the fighting is going on in the north of Sri Lanka," said Minister of the Environment and International Development Erik Solheim and stressed that the Sri Lankan government and LTTE have a responsibility to protect the civilian population and prevent more civilian deaths.

[*The Norwegian Government: "Unacceptable suffering among civilians in Sri Lanka"*, Ministry of Foreign Affairs, Norway, 27 January 2009 - www.regjeringen.no/en/dep/ud/press/News/2009/the-norwegian-government-unacceptable-su.html?id=543867]

28 January

According to the ICRC, hundreds of civilians were killed by the fighting in Sri Lanka. ICRC's head of South Asia operations, Jacques de Maio, said people were caught in the crossfire, hospitals and ambulances were hit by shelling and several aid workers were injured while evacuating the wounded. Medical facilities in the Vanni region of northern Sri Lanka were overwhelmed by hundreds of dead and scores of wounded from the fighting, which has intensified since the government took the last major LTTE held town of Mullaitivu on 25 January. He said his staff were forced to face the overwhelming influx of wounded and sick in hospitals which were themselves hit by shelling. The hospitals were under-equipped and under-staffed and suffered shortages of medical consumables.

[*ICRC warns of humanitarian crisis in Sri Lanka*, ABC News, 28 January 2009 - www.abc.net.au/news/stories/2009/01/28/2475976.htm?site=news]

29 January

Sri Lanka President Mahinda Rajapaksa said he was acutely conscious of the welfare of the civilians and called up on the LTTE to allow free movement of civilians within the next 48 hours to ensure their safety and security. He pledged a safe passage for all the civilians to a secure environment. He assured all people living in the north and conflict areas in particular, that vacating LTTE held areas will ensure their physical security and enable peace, freedom and rights for all citizens of Sri Lanka.

[*President urges LTTE: Release civilians in 48 hours*, News Line, Presidential Secretariat, 30 January 2009 www.priu.gov.lk/news_update/Current_Affairs/ca200901/20090130president_urges_ltte.htm]

January 2009

The UN and ICRC evacuated more than 200 civilians wounded by the fighting in the northern Vanni region, including 50 critically injured children. UN spokesman in Colombo, Gordon Weiss said, "However, this is by no means a full account of the casualties."

[*Sri Lanka: Civilians remain at risk in heavy fighting*, United Nations Office for the Coordination of Humanitarian Affairs - Integrated Regional Information Networks (IRIN), 30 January 2009 www.irinnews.org/Report.aspx?ReportId=82658]

At least 44 Tamil civilians were killed and 178 others were wounded by Sri Lanka army artillery shells at Suthanthirapuram and Iruddumadu in the Mullaitivu 'civilian safe zone'.

[*Artillery barrage kills 44 civilians, 178 wounded in 'safety zone'*, TamilNet, 29 January 2009 - www.tamilnet.com/art.html?catid=13&artid=28197]

UN High Commissioner for Human Rights Navi Pillay said in Geneva she was deeply concerned by reports of the rapidly deteriorating conditions facing a quarter of a million civilians trapped in the conflict zone in northern Sri Lanka, and of alleged human rights abuses and a significant number of civilian casualties, as well as the huge displacement. Ms. Pillay also expressed concern at the highly restricted access to the Vanni region for aid agencies and impartial outside observers, including journalists and human rights monitors. The High Commissioner cited reports of forced recruitment, including of children, as well as the use of civilians as human shields by the LTTE. She condemned the fact that 'civilian safe zones' promised by the government have subsequently been subjected to bombardment leading to civilian casualties. She said it is the government's duty to provide safety to all Sri Lanka's citizens, whatever their ethnic origin or political views, and that means not only protecting civilians during military operations in the north, but also ensuring space for journalists and human rights defenders to seek out the truth and expose abuses.

[*UN human rights chief deplores deteriorating situation for civilians in Sri Lanka*, UN Press Release, 29 January 2009 - www.unhchr.ch/huricane/huricane.nsf/view01/7C48F59856B2A8BCC125754D003C5D24?opendocument]

30 January

The UN warned that intense fighting in northern Sri Lanka continued to threaten civilian lives. UN spokesman in Colombo, Gordon Weiss said from the intensity of the fighting and the position of up to 300,000 civilians, including 230,000 IDPs, trapped in the Vanni, that non-combatants were being injured and killed. The safety of these people is the responsibility of both the warring parties. "The LTTE should also agree to it, but in all circumstances the government has a responsibility to protect the lives of its citizens – as it has consistently recognised", Mr Weiss added.

[*Sri Lanka: Civilians remain at risk in heavy fighting*, United Nations Office for the Coordination of Humanitarian Affairs - Integrated Regional Information Networks (IRIN), 30 January 2009 - www.irinnews.org/Report.aspx?ReportId=82658]

31 January

Moongilaru, Suthanthirapuram, Udaiyarkaddu, within the 'civilian safe zone' and Pokkanai and Puthukudyiruppu in Mullaitivu District were shelled by the army and bombed by the air force, killing 39 Tamil civilians and injuring 128 others.

[*Artillery-fired cluster shells, aerial bombing on safety zone, 39 civilians killed*, TamilNet, 31 January 2009 www.tamilnet.com/art.html?catid=13&artid=28237]

20

January 2009

The areas around Puthukudyiruppu Hospital in Mullaitivu District were shelled by the Sri Lanka army and shrapnel hit the hospital.

[*Sri Lanka Repeated shelling of hospitals evidence of war crimes*, Human Rights Watch, 8 May 2009 www.hrw.org/en/news/2009/05/08/sri-lanka-repeated-shelling-hospitals-evidence-war-crimes]

February 2009

1 February

The Sri Lanka army launched shell attacks three times on Puthukudyiruppu Hospital in Mullaitivu District causing damage. The ICRC said that the only functioning hospital in the combat zone was hit by shell fire killing nine people and wounding 20 others. Head of the ICRC Colombo delegation Paul Castella expressed shock that the hospital was hit for the second time in recent weeks.
[*Sri Lanka: Nine killed as hospital shelled – ICRC*, United Nations Office for the Coordination of Humanitarian Affairs - Integrated Regional Information Networks (IRIN), 2 February 2009 www.irinnews.org/Report.aspx?ReportId=82694; *Sri Lanka Repeated shelling of hospitals evidence of war crimes, Human Rights Watch, 8 May 2009   www.hrw.org/en/news/2009/05/08/sri-lanka-repeated-shelling-hospitals-evidence-war-crimes*]

2 February

The Sri Lanka army fired shells on the Kilinochchi makeshift hospital at Udaiyarkaddu killing a nurse.
[*Nurse killed in Udaiyarkaddu hospital, ICRC staff wounded in PTK*, TamilNet, 2 February 2009 www.tamilnet.com/art.html?catid=13&artid=28270]

The Sri Lanka army fired a shell at Puthukudyiruppu Hospital in Mullaitivu District, killing seven people including a nurse, and injuring 15 others.
[*Sri Lanka Repeated shelling of hospitals evidence of war crimes*, Human Rights Watch, 8 May 2009 www.hrw.org/en/news/2009/05/08/sri-lanka-repeated-shelling-hospitals-evidence-war-crimes]

The Sri Lanka Ministry of Defence issued the following statement: "While the Security Forces accept all responsibility to ensure the safety and protection of civilians in the Safety Zones, they are unable to give such an assurance to those who remain outside these zones. Therefore, the government, with full responsibility, urges all civilians to come to the Safety Zones; and also states that as civilians who do not heed this call will be among LTTE cadres, the Security Forces will not be able to accept responsibility for their safety."
[*Sri Lanka: Disregard for civilian safety appalling*, Human Rights Watch, 3 February 2009 - www.hrw.org/en/news/2009/02/03/sri-lanka-disregard-civilian-safety-appalling]

3 February

Two people were killed and several others were injured when the Sri Lanka army fired shells on Puthukudyiruppu Hospital in Mullaitivu District. The Operation Ward, Women Ward and the staff headquarters were damaged.
[*Sri Lanka Repeated shelling of hospitals evidence of war crimes*, Human Rights Watch, 8 May 2009 www.hrw.org/en/news/2009/05/08/sri-lanka-repeated-shelling-hospitals-evidence-war-crimes]

Brad Adams, Asia Director of Human Rights Watch (HRW) denounced Sri Lankan government statement that it is not responsible for the safety of civilians who remain in areas controlled by the LTTE as appalling disregard for the well-being of the civilian population and said it was contrary to international law. He said the government knows full well that civilians caught up in the current fighting are dangerously trapped, but shows callous indifference by saying civilians should not expect the government to consider their safety and security.
[*Sri Lanka: Disregard for civilian safety appalling*, Human Rights Watch, 3 February 2009 - www.hrw.org/en/news/2009/02/03/sri-lanka-disregard-civilian-safety-appalling]

February 2009

The Tokyo Co-Chairs (Norway, Japan, US and EU) urged on the Sri Lanka government and the LTTE not to fire out of or into the 'civilian safe zone' established by the government or in the vicinity of the Puthukudyiruppu Hospital (or any other medical structure), where more than 500 patients were receiving care and many hundreds more had sought refuge. The Co-Chairs also urged both sides to allow food and medical assistance to reach those trapped by fighting, cooperate with the ICRC to facilitate the evacuation of urgent medical cases, and ensure the safety of aid and medical workers.
[*Statement by the Tokyo Co-Chairs*, Tokyo Co-Chairs on Sri Lanka, 3 February 2009 - www.news.lk/index.php?option=com_content&task=view&id=8339&Itemid=44]

4 February

UN spokesman in Colombo, Gordon Weiss said that the Puthukudyiruppu Hospital in Mullaitivu District was under heavy artillery fire for about 18 hours, and cluster bombs were used on 4 February, which was a clear breach of humanitarian law. Sri Lanka is not a signatory to the 2008 UN Convention on Cluster Munitions, which prohibits all use, stockpiling, production and transfer of Cluster Munitions. But hospitals should not be targeted by any weapon under international humanitarian law. Mr. Weiss also said that 90% of the hospital's patients, who numbered 500 on 1 February 2009, had fled northwards but remained inside the conflict zone and had no access to medical facilities.
[*Wounded flee shelling of a hospital in Sri Lanka*, The New York Times, 4 February 2009 www.nytimes.com/2009/02/04/world/asia/04iht-05lanka.19917492.html; *Hillary Clinton and David Miliband call for Sri Lanka ceasefire with Tamils*, The Times (UK), 4 February 2009 www.timesonline.co.uk/tol/news/world/asia/article5657436.ece?print=yes&randnum=1151003209000]

5 February

The makeshift hospital at Udaiyarkaddu within the 'civilian safe zone' was shelled by the Sri Lanka army, killing seven Tamil civilians and injuring 27 others. Two ambulances and the medical store of the hospital were destroyed.
[*Hospital attacked, 7 killed, dozens wounded*, TamilNet, 5 February 2009 - www.tamilnet.com/art.html?catid=13&artid=28307]

The Sri Lanka government rejected the international call for a ceasefire saying troops would not suspend their offensive against the LTTE despite reports of a growing civilian death toll. The government said it would offer a limited amnesty to rebel forces that were ready to lay down their arms as they were on the brink of defeat. Defence Secretary Gotabaya Rajapaksa said that the international community should not expect the Sri Lankan government to allow the LTTE's participation as a political party in a fresh negotiations process after the armed forces crushed its wherewithal to wage war.
[*Sri Lanka rejects international call for ceasefire with Tamil Tigers*, Guardian (UK), 5 February 2009 - www.guardian.co.uk/world/2009/feb/05/sri-lanka-ceasefire-tamil-tigers]

6 February

The Sri Lanka air force bombed the Ponnampalam Memorial Hospital at Puthukudyiruppu in Mullaitivu District, killing 61 people within and outside the hospital.

February 2009

[*SLAF bombs Ponnampalam hospital, 61 patients killed*, TamilNet, 7 February 2009 –
www.tamilnet.com/art.html?catid=13&artid=28334, [*Sri Lanka Repeated shelling of hospitals evidence of war
crimes*, Human Rights Watch, 8 May 2009 - www.hrw.org/en/news/2009/05/08/sri-lanka-repeated-
shelling-hospitals-evidence-war-crimes]

7 February

The WFP warned that more than 250,000 civilians, trapped by fighting in the Vanni region of Sri
Lanka were facing a food crisis. The Vanni was practically sealed off to the outside world and the
civilians were totally dependent on international aid agencies which were unable to gain access to
the area. WFP spokeswoman, Emilia Casella, said the entire population of the Vanni faced a food
crisis due to continuous displacement, crop failure and recent floods. Their livelihood is almost
completely lost, exacerbating the food insecurity and their coping mechanisms have been exhausted.
The WFP wanted to send a food convoy into Vanni on 5 February (Thursday), but was unable to get
the necessary clearance from government officials, although the authorities had pledged WFP that
they would permit a humanitarian window of about four hours on Thursdays to send food into the
Vanni. Ms. Casella noted the last food convoy of WFP into the conflict zone was on 16 January 2009,
which would have satisfied the food needs only for about one week.
[*WFP: Thousands Face Food Crisis in Sri Lanka War Zone*, Voice of America, 7 February 2009 -
www1.voanews.com/english/news/a-13-2009-02-07-voa25-68811432.html]

At least 62 Tamil civilians were killed in Sri Lanka army shelling within the 'civilian safe zone' in
Suthanthirapuram, Iruddumadu, Udaiyarkaddu and Thevipuram in Mullaitivu District.
[*More than 180 killed in Sri Lankan bombardment within 48 hours*, TamilNet, 8 February 2009
www.tamilnet.com/art.html?catid=13&artid=28340]

A shell fired by the Sri Lanka army hit the makeshift hospital in Suthanthirapuram, Mullaitivu District
killing an employee of the hospital.
[*More than 180 killed in Sri Lankan bombardment within 48 hours*, TamilNet, 8 February 2009
www.tamilnet.com/art.html?catid=13&artid=28340]

9 February

Sri Lankan army shells killed 16 patients at the Puthumathalan makeshift hospital in Mullaitivu
District. Head of the ICRC delegation in Colombo Paul Castella said: "We are shocked that patients
are not afforded the protection they are entitled to. Once more, we call on both parties to meet
their obligation under international humanitarian law to spare wounded and sick people, medical
personnel and medical facilities at all times."
[*Sri Lanka: ICRC evacuates over 240 wounded and sick from the Vanni by sea*, ICRC, 10 February 2009
www.icrc.org/Web/Eng/siteeng0.nsf/html/sri-lanka-news-100209]

The ICRC evacuated 240 wounded and sick people from Puthumathalan in Mullaitivu District by sea
to Trincomalee. They included patients who fled from Puthukudyiruppu Hospital after it was
repeatedly shelled.
[*Sri Lanka: ICRC evacuates over 240 wounded and sick from the Vanni by sea*, ICRC, 10 February 2009 -
www.icrc.org/Web/Eng/siteeng0.nsf/html/sri-lanka-news-100209]

February 2009

Ten independent UN Experts expressed deep concern in Geneva at the deteriorating human rights situation in Sri Lanka, particularly the shrinking space for critical voices and the fear of reprisals against victims and witnesses which – together with a lack of effective investigations and prosecutions – has led to unabated impunity for human rights violations. A climate of fear and intimidation reigns over those defending human rights, especially over journalists and lawyers. The safety of defenders has worsened considerably over the past year, most significantly following denunciations of human rights abuses committed by parties to the conflict, of corruption by state officials and of impunity. Serious and fatal aggression against journalists and the media were a common occurrence. Notwithstanding the severity of the abuses in areas of conflict, the Experts highlighted that the problem is deeper and more endemic. The conflict deflects attention from the impunity which has been allowed to go unabated throughout Sri Lanka. The fear of reprisals against victims and witnesses, together with a lack of effective investigations and prosecutions, has led to a circle of impunity that must be broken. The Experts said they continue to receive disturbing reports of torture, extra-judicial killings and enforced disappearances throughout the country and called for an immediate end to impunity and reprisals.

The Experts were: (1) Special Rapporteur on human rights defenders, Margaret Sekaggya; (2) Special Rapporteur on freedom of opinion and expression, Frank La Rue; (3) Chairperson of the Working Group on Enforced or Involuntary Disappearances, Santiago Corcuera Cabezut; (4) Chairperson of the Working Group on Arbitrary Detention, Manuela Carmena Castrillo; (5) Special Rapporteur on the right of physical and mental health, Anand Grover; (6) Special Rapporteur on the independence of judges and lawyers, Leandro Despouy; (7) Special Rapporteur on the right to food, Olivier de Schutter; (8) Special Rapporteur on extrajudicial executions, Philip Alston; (9) Special Rapporteur on torture and degrading treatment, Manfred Nowak; (10) Special Rapporteur on adequate housing, Raquel Rolnik.

[*Sri Lanka: UN Experts deeply concerned at suppression of criticism and unabated impunity*, UN Press Release, 9 February 2009 -
www.unhchr.ch/huricane/huricane.nsf/view01/0D62B94306A51630C12575580053FECC?opendocume
nt]

12 February

The ICRC said it managed to evacuate 240 sick and injured civilians from Puthumathalan in Mullaitivu District to Trincomalee.

[*Tamil Tigers 'shoot' at civilians*, Al Jazeera, 12 February 2009
http://english.aljazeera.net/news/asia/2009/02/200921293030989823.html]

The LTTE shot and injured civilians as the ICRC tried to evacuate sick and wounded people by boat from Puthumathalan in Mullaitivu District. Sister Louise, a Catholic nun who attempted to steer civilians away from the fighting was wounded in the shooting. Other nuns said: "When we tried to leave, the LTTE didn't allow civilians to leave and said only we [the nuns] can leave ... so we stayed back with the civilians".

[*Tamil Tigers 'shoot' at civilians*, Al Jazeera, 12 February 2009
http://english.aljazeera.net/news/asia/2009/02/200921293030989823.html]

February 2009

The Sri Lankan security force headquarters in the Vanni declared a new 'civilian safe zone', with effect from 12 February 2009. The new safe zone is as follows: beginning from the northwest of Vadduvakal (09 17 26.60 N & 080 47 10.60 E) to the west, and north of Vadduvakal (09 18 06.08 N & 080 48 08.30 E) to the eastern coastal boundary, ran up to Palamathalan south (09 22 17.70 N & 080 42 35.60 E) on the western side. On the coastal belt up to the extreme north, the eastern strip ended at the southeast of Palamathalan (09 22 35.60 N & 080 42 53.80 E). The area between the northwest of Vadduvakal to the north of Vadduvakal that touches the eastern sea boundary was about 2 km in width and the extent at the northern end of the strip, touching Palamathalan area was about 1 km in breadth (Annex 3).

[*'No fire zone' declared further facilitating civilian safety*, Ministry of Defence, Sri Lanka, 12 February 2009 - www.defence.lk/new.asp?fname=20090212_09]

13 February

More than 50 Tamil civilians were feared killed at Thevipuram and Vallipunam in Mullaitivu District in Sri Lanka army artillery attacks.

[*75 feared killed in SLA shelling, elders home*, TamilNet, 14 February 2009 www.tamilnet.com/art.html?catid=13&artid=28418]

14 February

Fifteen Tamil civilians were killed and 35 others were wounded at Iranaippalai in Mullaitivu District in Sri Lanka army shell attacks. Four elders were killed and around 50 others were wounded when shells hit an elders' home.

[*75 feared killed in SLA shelling, elders home*, TamilNet, 14 February 2009 www.tamilnet.com/art.html?catid=13&artid=28418]

16 February

As more than 100,000 people fled from the old safe zone to the new 'civilian safe zone', the Sri Lanka army artillery fire targeted the roads leading to the new safe zone and the new zone itself. A large number of civilians were killed. Those killed included five humanitarian workers.

[*260 killed, SLA shells and boxes civilians, preventing movement to safer areas*, TamilNet, 16 February 2009 - www.tamilnet.com/art.html?catid=13&artid=28439]

The ICRC evacuated by ferry 440 patients and their families from Puthumathalan to Trincomalee, where they received medical treatment. Head of the ICRC delegation in Sri Lanka Paul Castella said: "Families continue to arrive in Puthumathalan in a state of utter exhaustion and despair, hoping to be treated and rescued. But the reality is that there is an almost complete lack of medicine and relief items there. We did save lives today but many people remain behind, helpless and anxiously waiting to be evacuated. It is now a matter of life and death."

[*Sri Lanka: ICRC evacuates more sick and wounded from the Vanni*, ICRC, 16 February 2009 www.icrc.org/Web/Eng/siteeng0.nsf/html/sri-lanka-news-160209]

17 February

Fifteen Tamil civilians fleeing from the old safe zone to the new 'civilian safe zone' were killed in Sri Lanka army artillery fire.

[*SLA artillery fire hits new 'safety zone', 108 killed, 200 wounded*, TamilNet, 18 February 2009 - www.tamilnet.com/art.html?catid=13&artid=28449]

February 2009

18 February

Sri Lanka army artillery fire targeted areas within the new 'civilian safe zone', including Mathalan, Pokkanai and Mullivaikkal, killing 108 Tamil civilians and injuring more than 200 others. Artillery attacks were also launched on Thevipuram and Vallipunam in the old safe zone, trapping thousands of civilians and preventing them moving to the new zone.

[*SLA artillery fire hits new 'safety zone', 108 killed, 200 wounded*, TamilNet, 18 February 2009 www.tamilnet.com/art.html?catid=13&artid=28449]

The Sri Lanka air force bombed IDPs at Ananthapuram in Iranaipalai, Mullaitivu District killing at least 50 Tamil civilians and wounding some 70 others. Ten of the injured died while being taken to Mathalan hospital. More than 180 shelters were destroyed in the bombardment.

[*Massive air attack on civilian targets, scores killed*, TamilNet, 18 February 2009 www.tamilnet.com/art.html?catid=13&artid=28451; *30 families wiped out in massive attack Wednesday, shelling continues*, TamilNet, 19 February 2009, - www.tamilnet.com/art.html?catid=13&artid=28470]

19 February

Sri Lanka army shell attacks killed 24 Tamil civilians in Puthukudyiruppu in Mullaitivu District. Ten people were killed in Iranaipalai, Ananthapuram and Valaiyanmadam.

[*30 families wiped out in massive attack Wednesday, shelling continues*, TamilNet, 19 February 2009, - www.tamilnet.com/art.html?catid=13&artid=28470]

20 February

Sri Lanka army artillery attacks targeted Mathalan, Pokkanai, Valaiyanmadam and Iranaipalai in Mullaitivu District and injured 70 Tamil civilians within the 'civilian safe zone' and surrounding areas. Thirteen of the wounded civilians died in Mathalan hospital.

[*13 civilians killed, 70 wounded in SLA barrage Friday night*, TamilNet, 21 February 2009 www.tamilnet.com/art.html?catid=13&artid=28484]

Two LTTE planes bombed the headquarters of the Inland Revenue Department in Colombo, killing two people and injuring 38 others. The military said one of the aircrafts was shot down near Katunayake airport.

[*LTTE planes bomb Sri Lankan capital*, Global Security, 21 February 2009 - www.globalsecurity.org/military/library/news/2009/02/mil-090221-irna04.htm]

21 February

Thirty three Tamil civilians were killed and 73 others were injured in Sri Lanka army artillery attacks, including in the 'civilian safe zone' areas of Valaiyanmadam, Mullivaikal, and Pokkanai. Fourteen of the wounded died in the makeshift hospital at Mathalan.

[*50 Tamil civilians killed, 130 wounded within 48 hours*, TamilNet, 22 February 2009 - www.tamilnet.com/art.html?catid=13&artid=28498]

22 February

Sri Lanka army attacks killed 20 Tamil civilians and wounded 60 others in Iranaipalai, Ananthapuram and Puthukudyiruppu in Mullaitivu District. There were many children among the wounded.

February 2009

[*50 Tamil civilians killed, 130 wounded within 48 hours*, TamilNet, 22 February 2009 - www.tamilnet.com/art.html?catid=13&artid=28498]

24 February

Sri Lanka army artillery fire killed six Tamil IDP civilians, including two children, at Puthumathalan within the 'civilian safe zone' in Mullaitivu District.

[*Children vulnerable to SLA shelling in new 'safe zone'*, TamilNet, 24 February 2009 - www.tamilnet.com/art.html?catid=13&artid=28515]

28 February

Forty Tamil civilians were killed at Mullivaikal, Valaiyanmadam, Pokkanai, Mathalan in Mullaitivu District within the 'civilian safe zone' in Sri Lanka army shell attacks and air force bombardment.

[*SLA shelling kills 122 within 3 days in Mullaitivu*, TamilNet, 2 March 2009 - www.tamilnet.com/art.html?catid=13&artid=28574]

March 2009

1 March

Thirty seven Tamil civilians were killed in the 'civilian safe zone' areas of Mullivaikal, Valaiyanmadam, Pokkanai and Mathalan in Mullaitivu District in Sri Lanka army shell attacks.
[*SLA shelling kills 122 within 3 days in Mullaitivu*, TamilNet, 2 March 2009
www.tamilnet.com/art.html?catid=13&artid=28574]

2 March

Sri Lanka army artillery shells killed 45 Tamil civilians in Iranaipalai and the 'civilian safe zone' areas of Mullivaikal, Valaiyanmadam, Pokkanai and Mathalan in Mullaitivu District.
[*SLA shelling kills 122 within 3 days in Mullaitivu*, TamilNet, 2 March 2009 -
www.tamilnet.com/art.html?catid=13&artid=28574]

In a letter to Mullaitivu Government Agent, Regional Health Services Director Dr T. Varatharajah said as follows: "You are aware that the people are facing death by starvation because of the ongoing war. In the last few days the bodies of 13 people who had died of starvation were brought to our hospital. Of them, five people have been identified. Because of the rise in prices and non-availability of food, most people are eating leaves and food they are not accustomed to. Six members of a family who ate leaves they are not accustomed to, have been admitted to the hospital in an unconscious state."
[*RDHS confirms 13 hunger deaths, urges officials to act*, TamilNet, 3 March 2009
www.tamilnet.com/art.html?catid=13&artid=28592]

3 March

Sri Lanka army and air force attacks killed 73 Tamil civilians and wounded more than 160 others, most of them inside the 'civilian safe zone', at Mathalan, Pokkanai, Iranaipalai and Mullivaikal in Mullaitivu District. The dead included at least 11 children. Thirteen people were killed and 56 others were injured when the Sri Lanka army fired artillery shells on IDP settlements near the makeshift hospital in Mathalan.
[*SLA shells hospital environs, 13 killed including 4 children*, TamilNet, 3 March 2009 -
www.tamilnet.com/art.html?catid=13&artid=28591; *SLA in killing spree in the 'safety zone'*, 73 killed, 160 wounded, TamilNet, 4 March 2009 - www.tamilnet.com/art.html?catid=13&artid=28597]

4 March

ICRC Staff member Vadivel Vijayakumar was killed by shell fire north of Valaiyanmadam, in Mullaitivu District. His nine year-old son was injured. Mr. Vijayakumar was involved in ICRC-facilitated medical evacuations, helping to bring patients from the makeshift medical facility in Puthumathalan to the beach and then on to the ICRC ferry for evacuation to Trincomalee.
[*Sri Lanka: ICRC staff member killed in the conflict area*, ICRC, 5 March 2009 -
www.icrc.org/Web/Eng/siteeng0.nsf/html/sri-lanka-news-050309]

Sri Lanka army artillery fire killed 78 Tamil civilians including 21 children, and injured 182 others in the 'civilian safe zone' areas of Pokkanai, Mathalan, and Mullivaikal in Mullaitivu District.
[*SLA shelling kills more children, carnage in 'safety zone'*, TamilNet, 4 March 2009 -
www.tamilnet.com/art.html?catid=13&artid=28603]

March 2009

5 March

Kilinochchi Regional Director of Health Services (RDHS) Dr. Thangamuthu Sathiyamoorthy said in a report that only 109.71 metric tonnes (MT) (2.2%) of food had been received in February 2009 through ICRC ships, while the requirement per month was 4950 MT. According to the Government Agent's statement of 28 February 2009, around 330,000 persons from about 81,000 families were living in and around the 'civilian safe zone' in Mullaitivu District and more than 90% of the people lived in tarpaulin shelters. The report said that people faced starvation. Children, women, elders and those seriously ill were particularly vulnerable to the onslaught of starvation unless the food condition is urgently rectified. According to the report, 13 people had died of starvation in the latter part of February alone.

[*Only 2.2% of humanitarian supplies reached Vanni in February* – RDHS, TamilNet, 6 March 2009 - www.tamilnet.com/art.html?catid=13&artid=28617]

Sixty nine Tamil civilians were killed in shelling by the Sri Lanka army and bombing by the Sri Lanka air force in Iranaipalai, Mullivaikal and Valaiyanmadam in Mullaitivu District.

[*Sri Lankan attacks kill 208 civilians within 72 hours*, TamilNet, 7 March 2009 - www.tamilnet.com/art.html?catid=13&artid=28639]

6 March

Eighty six Tamil civilians were killed and more than 100 others were wounded in military attacks in the Vanni.

[*Sri Lankan attacks kill 208 civilians within 72 hours*, TamilNet, Saturday, 07 March 2009 www.tamilnet.com/art.html?catid=13&artid=28639]

7 March

Fifty three Tamil civilians were killed and 112 others were injured when the Sri Lanka army fired artillery shells on IDP settlements in Ambalavanpokkanai and Mathalan within the 'civilian safe zone' in Mullaitivu District.

[*Sri Lankan attacks kill 208 civilians within 72 hours*, TamilNet, 7 March 2009 www.tamilnet.com/art.html?catid=13&artid=28639]

8 March

Sri Lanka army shell attacks killed 49 Tamil civilians in the 'civilian safe zone' in Mullaitivu District, including in Mathalan.

[*Shelling amidst mini-cyclone and lashing rains, thousands stranded*, TamilNet, 9 March 2009 www.tamilnet.com/art.html?catid=13&artid=28661]

9 March

The Sri Lanka army fired shells into the 'civilian safe zone' killing 56 Tamil civilians, including 18 children, and injuring more than 100 others. The attacks were launched on Ambalavanpokkanai, Pachchaippulmoddai, Valaiyanmadam, Mathalan, Iraddaivaikal and Mullivaikal in Mullaitivu District.

[*Colombo's shelling carnage of flood-hit civilians, 25 children killed*, TamilNet, Tuesday, 10 March 2009 www.tamilnet.com/art.html?catid=13&artid=28665]

March 2009

10 March

The Sri Lankan army attacked the 'civilian safe zone' in Mullaitivu District including Mathalan, Dharmapuram and Valaiyanmadam with cluster bombs. Eighty six Tamil civilians, including 49 children, were killed. Another 47 people died on the way or after admission to the hospital. Two hundred and seventy three civilians were wounded. Mathalan Village Officer (Grama Sevaka) Pulendran and ICRC worker V. Vincent were among the injured.

[*SLA shelling kills 133 civilians including 49 children on Tuesday*, TamilNet, 11 March 2009 www.tamilnet.com/art.html?catid=13&artid=28689]

11 March

Eighty two Tamil civilians were killed and more than 130 others were wounded by Sri Lanka army shells and air force bombing in Mullivaikal, Mathalan, Valaiyanmadam and Pokkanai inside the 'civilian safe zone' in Mulliativu District. According to the RDHS, the makeshift hospital in Puthumathalan received 964 civilian casualties in the first ten days of March 2009. The RDHS said: "Almost all the cases were victims of intense shelling. A few of the victims were due to the aerial attacks and gunshot injuries. More than 95% of the victims were from the safe area and 40 children and 79 adults died while being taken to the hospital or during the treatment or after having been treated".

[*SLA shelling kills 82 civilians inside 'safe zone' on Wednesday*, TamilNet, 12 March 2009 www.tamilnet.com/art.html?catid=13&artid=28699]

12 March

Sixty two civilians were killed and 129 others were wounded in Mathalan, Valaiyanmadam and Mullivaikal within the 'civilian safe zone', in Sri Lanka army shelling.

[*SLA shelling targets humanitarian supplies in 'safe zone'*, TamilNet, 13 March 2009 www.tamilnet.com/art.html?catid=13&artid=28701]

13 March

US Secretary of State Hillary Clinton called Sri Lankan President Mahinda Rajapaksa over the telephone to express deep concern over the deteriorating conditions and increasing loss of life in the government-designated 'civilian safe zone' in northern Sri Lanka. Secretary Clinton stated that the Sri Lankan army should not fire into the civilian areas of the conflict zone. She condemned the LTTE for holding civilians as human shields, and shooting at civilians leaving LTTE-controlled areas. She urged the President to give international humanitarian relief organizations full access to the conflict area and displaced persons camps, including screening centres.

[*Humanitarian Situation in Sri Lanka*, Bureau of Public Affairs, US State Department, 13 March 2009 - www.state.gov/r/pa/prs/ps/2009/03/120341.htm]

Thirty one Tamil civilians were killed by Sri Lanka army artillery shells in the 'civilian safe zone' areas of Valaiyanmadam, Iraddaivaikal, Mullivaikal and Mathalan. Shells exploded near the makeshift hospital in Puthumathalan inside the 'civilian safe zone' causing further injuries to four patients who were already wounded.

[*SLA shelling targets relief supplies and hospital, patients wounded*, TamilNet, 13 March 2009 www.tamilnet.com/art.html?catid=13&artid=28709]

March 2009

The UN High Commissioner for Human Rights Navi Pillay expressed her growing alarm at the increasing number of civilians reported killed and injured in the conflict in northern Sri Lanka, and at the apparent ruthless disregard being shown for their safety. She said that certain actions by the Sri Lankan military and by the LTTE may constitute violations of international human rights and humanitarian law, and that the world today is ever sensitive about such acts that could amount to war crimes and crimes against humanity. OHCHR said sources indicated that more than 2,800 civilians may have been killed and over 7,000 injured since 20 January 2009. Even after the Sri Lankan government's announcement on 24 February 2009 that heavy weapons would no longer be fired into the 'civilian safe zones', close to 500 people were reportedly killed and more than a thousand injured in these zones. Of these deaths, the great majority have been attributed to the use of heavy weapons. Overall, since 20 January, more than two thirds of the reported deaths and injuries have occurred in the 'civilian safe zones'.

OHCHR also said that the LTTE are reported to be continuing to hold civilians as human shields, to have shot at civilians trying to leave the area they control and they are also believed to have been forcibly recruiting civilians, including children, as soldiers. The High Commissioner called on both the Sri Lankan government and the LTTE to immediately suspend hostilities in order to allow the evacuation of the entire civilian population by land or sea. She also urged the Sri Lankan government to grant full access to UN and other independent agencies to allow an accurate assessment of the human rights and humanitarian conditions in the conflict zone.

[*Serious violations of international law committed in Sri Lanka conflict: UN human rights chief*, UN Press release, 13 March 2009   www2.ohchr.org/english/press/newsFrameset-2.htm]

14 March

The Sri Lanka army and the air force continued to target areas within the 'civilian safe zone' such as Mathalan, Mullivaikal and Iraddaivaikal in Mullaitivu District, killing 69 Tamil civilians, including 19 children. Twenty nine of them were killed near the makeshift hospital in Mathalan.

[*Civilian casualties mount as intense bombing and shelling continues*, TamilNet15 March 2009 - www.tamilnet.com/art.html?catid=13&artid=28722]

15 March

Fifty eight Tamil civilians were killed in Sri Lanka army shelling in Mullaitivu District.

['*Safe zone' under encircling fire, 137 killed in 3 days, ICRC worker wounded*, TamilNet, 17 March 2009 - www.tamilnet.com/art.html?catid=13&artid=28743]

16 March

A rocket-propelled grenade killed two people in the Puthumathalan makeshift hospital in Mullaitivu District.

[*Sri Lanka Repeated shelling of hospitals evidence of war crimes*, Human Rights Watch, 8 May 2009 www.hrw.org/en/news/2009/05/08/sri-lanka-repeated-shelling-hospitals-evidence-war-crimes]

In a letter to the Secretary to the Sri Lanka Ministry of Healthcare and Nutrition, the RDHSs of Mullaitivu and Kilinochchi, Dr. Thurairajah Varatharajah and Dr. Thangamuthu Sathiyamoorthy said that lack of medical supplies has led to the needless deaths of hundreds of hospital patients. The two districts had not been provided adequate supplies of essential medicines for the previous four

March 2009

months. The last supply of drugs and dressings was for the fourth quarter of 2008 and that too less than 5% of the combined quota for the two districts had been received. The rest of the medical supplies were kept at Vavuniya awaiting security clearance from the Ministry of Defence, despite repeated requests from the RDHSs directly to the Health Secretary and through the Provincial Director of Health Services by all available means of communication.

The RDHSs said further: "As the ongoing battle became more and more intense since the last months of last year, the number of war wounded has been steadily increasing with proportionate increase in the demand for essential medicines, especially anaesthetics, antibiotics, analgesics and IV fluids. Since January 2009, more than 500 civilian deaths, either on or after admission, have been registered at hospitals and thousands of civilian deaths could have gone unrecorded as they were not brought to the hospitals. Most of them succumbed to the war wounds. Some were due to serious medical illnesses. Most of the hospital deaths could have been prevented if basic infrastructure facilities and essential medicines were made available. The few Medical Officers and other health staff serving with dedication and determination have been frustrated of this grave situation of not being able to save lives. We have been supplied with no antibiotics, no anaesthetics and not a single bottle of IV fluid, leaving us in a desperate situation of not being able to providing even lifesaving emergency surgery.

"Furthermore we are unable to provide basic out-patients care, primary healthcare services and other institutionalized healthcare services due to the non-availability of essential medicines. This has already led to deaths of children and vulnerable elderly due to diarrhoea and other serious infections.

"Therefore any further delay in sending essential medicines would only cause more and more deaths of innocent civilians. We have urged for urgent sending of drugs and dressing several times during the past weeks and, in fact, yourself and Provincial Director have promised us to send urgent medical items in the ship when it came here last time. However, we were shocked and felt very sad when were informed by ICRC that no medicines have been handed over by the ministry officials to be taken in the ship.

"Hence we would be grateful if you could send the required medicines at least in the next ICRC chartered ship in order to save the lives of innocent civilians who are under constant threat of war."
[*Allow ICRC to transport medicines, RDHS urge Sri Lankan Health Ministry*, TamilNet, 17 March 2009 www.tamilnet.com/art.html?catid=13&artid=28741]

Sri Lanka army shell attacks and gunfire killed 35 Tamil civilians within the 'civilian safe zone' in Mullaitivu District, and wounded 73 others. ICRC worker, K. Pulenthirarasa, was wounded by gunfire near Mathalan hospital. Fifty two civilians, including 12 children, were admitted to the hospital. Five of the wounded died after admission.
[*'Safe zone' under encircling fire, 137 killed in 3 days, ICRC worker wounded*, TamilNet, 17 March 2009 - www.tamilnet.com/art.html?catid=13&artid=28743]

March 2009

17 March

Sri Lanka air force bombs and army shelling that targeted Pachchaippulmoddai and Valaiyanmadam within the 'civilian safe zone' killed 52 Tamil civilians and injured 182 others.

[*84 killed, 182 wounded in SLAF attacks, shelling on Tuesday*, TamilNet, 17 March 2009 www.tamilnet.com/art.html?catid=13&artid=28748]

18 March

A leaked document of the UN Office of the Humanitarian Coordinator in Sri Lanka of March 2009 said: "Total number of civilian casualties since 20 January 2009, as of 7 March 2009 in the conflict area of Mullaitivu District: 9,924 people including 2,683 deaths and 7,241 injuries (The ratio of death vs. injuries is estimated to be 35.5%).

"The number of people killed each day has doubled in one month. Attempts were made to indicate children under 15 years as an indicator of the presence of civilian casualties in general. Only partial figures were accumulated due to the difficulty of obtaining a constant breakdown. Nevertheless there are at least 135 deaths, 707 injuries since 20 January. However like the basic casualty figure itself, this is thought to be a gross under estimate. Based on the population assumption[1] the figure is likely to be closer to 400 deaths, and 1,100 injured. The recruitment of children by the LTTE must now be factored into the numbers of children who will perish.

"Between January and February 2009 the combat area was reduced from 100 km^2 to 45km^2 including the NFZ (No Fire Zone) of 14 km^2. As the combat area reduces the daily average shows an increase in the number of people killed (from 33 to 63) and a slight decrease in the number of injured (from 184 to 145). This is due to increased density, the use of heavy weapons which continue to strike the NFZ, and inadequate medical treatment".

[*Civilian casualties in the Vanni*, UN Office of the Resident Coordinator and Humanitarian Coordinator, March 2009 - www.innercitypress.com/3832_001.pdf]

At least 17 Tamil civilians were reported killed inside the 'civilian safe zone' in Mullaitivu District.

[*SLA shelling kills 102 civilians within 3 days inside 'safety zone'*, TamilNet, 21 March 2009 - www.tamilnet.com/art.html?catid=13&artid=28788]

A second leaked document of the UN Office of the Humanitarian Coordinator in Sri Lanka of March 2009 said that according to the UN and the ICRC, the number of IDPs in Mullaitivu was 150,000-190,000, while according to the Sri Lankan government it was 70,000. Regarding food supply to the Vanni, the document further said:

"18,217 MT – total food quantity delivered by road into the Vanni between September 2008 and January 2009 (average of 3,639 MT per month).

"There was a gap of two weeks after the end of January.

"150 MT – monthly food shipments in February 2009 by boat. This represents 4.1% of the average delivered by road in previous months.

---

[1] The preparation of each new revision of the official population estimates and projections of the UN involves the formulation of detailed assumptions about the future paths of fertility, mortality and international migration *World Population Prospects: The 2008 Revision*, UN Population Division - http://esa.un.org/UNPP/index.asp?panel=4

March 2009

"224 MT – Food shipments in March 2009 by boat. This represents 7% of the monthly average delivered by road in previous months.

"20,000 people – number of IDPs that current food supply supports per month [based on WFP figure of 500g per person per day] but excluding the negative effects of one month without regular delivery. Food stocks are on standby outside the Vanni but delivery of required food to IDPs is restricted by GOSL access. The latest negotiation with the Government allowed 500 MT mixed food commodities to be dispatched, using the sea.

"<u>We need to send to the NFZ at least 3,000 MT of food per month for a caseload of 200,000 people.</u>

"After several weeks of reports of food shortages, it's highly predicted that mortality could set in as a significant number of IDP population is reportedly weakened and the likelihood of malnutrition across the same population group could translate into a rapid increase of nutritional and health deterioration. A recent report from Mullaitivu also stressed the seriousness of the food situation in Mullaitivu that people's nutritional condition shows significant deterioration.

"Reports indicate that only limited stock was transferred to the new NFZ and that limited food reserves that some IDPs carried into the coastal strip are becoming depleted.

"High congestion, lack of sanitation and access to clean water for many and a reduced availability of firewood to facilitate food preparation and cooking will be factors that further contribute to the deterioration of health conditions."

[*Food delivery to IDPs in the Vanni*, UN Office of the Resident Coordinator and Humanitarian Coordinator, March 2009   www.innercitypress.com/3833_001.pdf]

19 March
Thirty nine Tamil civilians including 11 children were killed in heavy shelling in Pokkanai and Mathalan areas within the 'civilian safe zone' in Mullaitivu District.
[*SLA shelling kills 102 civilians within 3 days inside 'safety zone'*, TamilNet, 21 March 2009
www.tamilnet.com/art.html?catid=13&artid=28788]

20 March
Sri Lanka army shelling killed 46 civilians in Pokkanai, Mullivaikkal, Iraddaivaikkal, and Valaiyanmadam within the 'civilian safe zone' in Mullaitivu District.
[*SLA shelling kills 102 civilians within 3 days inside 'safety zone'*, TamilNet, 21 March 2009 -
www.tamilnet.com/art.html?catid=13&artid=28788]

21 March
The Sri Lanka army fired shells into the 'civilian safe zone' in Mullaitivu District, killing 42 Tamil civilians and causing injuries to around 80 others. Seven civilians who went to Iranaipalai to collect coconuts were reported killed in an air strike.
[*42 civilians killed, 80 wounded in Vanni Saturday*, TamilNet, 22 March 2009
www.tamilnet.com/art.html?catid=13&artid=28793]

23 March
A rocket-propelled grenade (RPG) killed a child near the Puthumathalan makeshift hospital in Mullaitivu District. Two shells injured 15 people near the hospital.

March 2009

[*Sri Lanka Repeated shelling of hospitals evidence of war crimes*, Human Rights Watch, 8 May 2009 - www.hrw.org/en/news/2009/05/08/sri-lanka-repeated-shelling-hospitals-evidence-war-crimes]

Sri Lanka army mortar shelling, RPG attacks and gunfire killed 96 Tamil civilians, including 19 children, in Mathalan, Puthumathalan and Pokkanai, within the 'civilian safe zone' in Mullaitivu District. Around 160 other civilians were wounded.
[*SLA attacks kill 128 civilians in 48 hours*, TamilNet, 24 March 2009 - www.tamilnet.com/art.html?catid=13&artid=28810]

24 March

Sri Lanka army shelling targeted Pokkanai, Ampalavanpokkanai, Mullivaikal, Mathalan and Valaiyanmadam, while the air force heavily bombed settlements around Pachchaipulmoddai within the 'civilian safe zone' in Mullaitivu District. Sixty two Tamil civilians were killed and many were injured.
[*62 civilians killed, SLA, SLAF step up attacks on safety zone*, TamilNet, 24 March 2009 www.tamilnet.com/art.html?catid=13&artid=28820]

The ICRC said it had evacuated by sea, with the help of the Sri Lankan navy, more than 5,000 sick and wounded civilians and caregivers from Puthumathalan in Mullaitivu District to government-controlled Trincomalee town, since 10 February 2009. On 22 March 2009, more than 490 patients and caregivers were evacuated.
[*Sri Lanka: Thousands flee conflict-hit north*, UN Office for the Coordination of Humanitarian Affairs – Integrated Regional Information Networks (IRIN), 24 March 2009 - www.irinnews.org/Report.aspx?ReportId=83598]

UN spokesman in Colombo, Gordon Weiss said that the UN has not received any response to the request to the LTTE to release two UN local staff members and three dependents, including a 16-year-old girl, forcibly recruited. The two staff members and the dependents were recruited in March 2009 and the UN officially protested to the LTTE on 16 March 2009 and requested they be released immediately.
[*Sri Lanka: Thousands flee conflict-hit north*, UN Office for the Coordination of Humanitarian Affairs – Integrated Regional Information Networks (IRIN), 24 March 2009 - www.irinnews.org/Report.aspx?ReportId=83598]

25 March

Hundred and thirty one Tamil civilians, including 32 children, were killed in attacks by the Sri Lanka army and the air force inside the 'civilian safe zone' in Mullaitivu District. The dead included humanitarian workers Ms. Mariyanayagam Daisyrani, 52, of the Mullaitivu District Government Secretariat and Ms. Janoja, 27, engaged in delivering humanitarian aid for the WFP. Two hundred and fifty two people, including 49 children were wounded. The attacks took place between Puthumathalan and Valaiyanmadam.
[*Carnage continues, 131 civilians including 32 children killed Wednesday*, TamilNet, 26 March 2009 - www.tamilnet.com/art.html?catid=13&artid=28838; *SLA attacks kill Mullai DS officials engaged in humanitarian work*, TamilNet, 26 March 2009 www.tamilnet.com/art.html?catid=13&artid=28840]

March 2009

26 March

The Sri Lanka army attacked the makeshift hospital at Puthumathalan with RPG killing five patients who were being treated at the intensive care unit, and injuring 11 others, including two medical staff. Six patients who were being treated for shell attack injuries were wounded again. The attack also destroyed part of the medicines in the hospital.

[*SLA attacks hospital, 5 patients killed, 11 wounded*, TamilNet, 26 March 2009
www.tamilnet.com/art.html?catid=13&artid=28839]

The Sri Lanka army fired shells on IDP shelters in Valaiyanmadam and Pokkanai killing 59 Tamil civilians. Village Officer (Grama Sevaka) Ms. Ajantha Abarajithan was among those killed in Valaiyanmadam.

[*179 civilians including 76 children killed within 3 days inside 'safety zone'*, TamilNet, 28 March 2009 -
www.tamilnet.com/art.html?catid=13&artid=28864]

27 March

Sixty three Tamil civilians, including 21 children, were killed in Sri Lanka army shell attacks between Mathalan and Pokkanai within the 'civilian safe zone' in Mullaitivu District. ICRC worker, P. Satheeskumar, was among the wounded.

[*179 civilians including 76 children killed within 3 days inside 'safety zone'*, TamilNet, 28 March 2009 -
www.tamilnet.com/art.html?catid=13&artid=28864]

28 March

Sri Lanka army attacks killed 57 Tamil civilians in Mullaitivu District.

[*179 civilians including 76 children killed within 3 days inside 'safety zone'*, TamilNet, 28 March 2009 -
www.tamilnet.com/art.html?catid=13&artid=28864]

29 March

Sri Lanka army artillery, mortar and long-distance gunfire killed 53 Tamil civilians and injured 119 others. The deaths took place in Mathalan, Pokkanai, Valaiyanmadam and Pachchaippulmoddai in Mullaitivu District. Around 1,190 people including 275 children, belonging to 298 families lost their shelters in five days of army attacks.

[*SLA attacks kill 53 civilians inside 'safety zone' Sunday*, TamilNet, 30 March 2009 -
www.tamilnet.com/art.html?catid=13&artid=28878]

30 March

The Sri Lanka army launched shell attacks on IDP settlements in Iraddaivaikal, Mullivaikal and Valaiyanmadam in Mullaitivu District killing 88 Tamil civilians, including 21 children, and wounding 156 others of whom 31 were children. Sixty three tarpaulin shelters and six shops were destroyed.

[*SLA attacks kill 88 Tamils, including 21 children on Monday*, TamilNet, 31 March 2009
www.tamilnet.com/art.html?catid=13&artid=28889]

31 March

Sri Lanka army shelling killed 43 civilians, including three children, and wounded 120 others in Mullaitivu District. The attacks took place in the 'civilian safe zone', including in Ampalavanpokkanai and Valaiyanmadam.

March 2009

[*SLA fires cluster shells, 45 civilians killed, 120 wounded Tuesday*, TamilNet, 31 March 2009
www.tamilnet.com/art.html?catid=13&artid=28891]

In a report titled "A Profile of Human Rights and Humanitarian Issues in the Vanni and Vavuniya", Sri
Lankan NGO, the Centre for Policy Alternatives (CPA) said that reports based on interviews of IDPs
who had fled the Vanni made clear that those attempting to flee have had to face serious
repercussions. The LTTE shot at civilians who attempted to leave, injuring some in the legs,
shoulders and arms.
[*A Profile of Human Rights and Humanitarian Issues in the Vanni and Vavuniya*, Centre for Policy Alternatives,
March 2009   http://www.internal-
displacement.org/idmc/website/countries.nsf/(httpEnvelopes)/F1A0A3A430C2C51BC12575A6005B8
EAC?OpenDocument]

April 2009

1 April

Thirty three Tamil civilians were killed and 78 others were wounded in Sri Lanka army attacks in the 'civilian safe zone' in Mullaitivu District.

[*SLA attacks kill 90 civilians within 3 days, 195 wounded*, TamilNet, 3 April 2009
www.tamilnet.com/art.html?catid=13&artid=28933]

2 April

Sri Lanka army attacks killed 31 Tamil civilians and injured 70 others in the 'civilian safe zone' in Mullaitivu District.

[*SLA attacks kill 90 civilians within 3 days, 195 wounded*, TamilNet, 3 April 2009 -
www.tamilnet.com/art.html?catid=13&artid=28933]

3 April

Twenty six Tamil civilians were killed in the 'civilian safe zone' in Sri Lanka army attacks. Forty seven injured civilians were admitted to the makeshift hospital in Puthumathalan.

[*SLA attacks kill 90 civilians within 3 days, 195 wounded*, TamilNet, 3 April 2009 -
www.tamilnet.com/art.html?catid=13&artid=28933]

4 April

Sri Lanka army attacks killed 71 civilians and wounded 143 others in the 'civilian safe zone' in Mullaitivu District.

[*SLA intensifies attacks on Safe Zone, 71 civilians killed*, 143 wounded, TamilNet, 5 April 2009 -
www.tamilnet.com/art.html?catid=13&artid=28950]

6 April

Forty three Tamil civilians were killed and 102 others sustained injuries in Sri Lanka army attacks in the 'civilian safe zone' in Mullaitivu District.

[*SLA bombs child nutrition centre in safety zone, 258 including 100 children wounded*, TamilNet, 8 April 2009 -
www.tamilnet.com/art.html?catid=13&artid=28975]

7 April

The head of mission of Medecins Sans Frontieres (MSF) Anne Marie Loof estimated that there were 150,000 people crammed into a 20km square stretch of coastline and jungle in Mullaitivu District. They had extremely basic shelter and did not have enough food, drinking water or medicines and were living in water up to their knees following monsoon rains. She said they were surrounded by continuous fighting, smoke, shelling and bombing and spent a lot of time lying down in ditches.

[*MSF head of mission speaks out on Sri Lanka*, Medecins Sans Frontieres, 7 April 2009 -
www.msf.org.uk/interview_head_of_mission_sri_lanka_20090407.news]

Sri Lanka army attacks killed 21 Tamil civilians in the 'civilian safe zone' in Mullaitivu District and injured 62 others.

[*SLA bombs child nutrition centre in safety zone, 258 including 100 children wounded*, TamilNet, 8 April 2009
www.tamilnet.com/art.html?catid=13&artid=28975]

April 2009

According to a doctor at the makeshift hospital in Puthumathalan, in Mullaitivu District, the hospital received 133 wounded civilians and 20 dead bodies, all victims of shelling in Pokkanai, within the 'civilian safe zone'.
[*Sri Lanka: Stop Shelling 'No-Fire Zone'*, Human Rights Watch, 9 April 2009
www.hrw.org/en/news/2009/04/09/sri-lanka-stop-shelling-no-fire-zone]

8 April
Human rights group Tamils Against Genocide (TAG) organized a rally of Tamils in New York City before the Indian, Mexican and the US missions to the UN, intended to show the urgency of stopping the slaughter of Tamil civilians by the Sri Lankan armed forces in northern Sri Lanka. TAG urged the international community to act immediately to stop the imminent massacre and aid hundreds of thousands of trapped Tamil civilians.
[*Tamil massacre imminent: Human rights group Tamils Against Genocide*, Reuters, 8 April 2009 -
www.reuters.com/article/pressRelease/idUS148963+08-Apr-2009+MW20090408]

In a discussion with US-based organizations representing the Tamil Diaspora, US Assistant Secretary of State for South and Central Asian Affairs Richard Boucher and US Ambassador to Sri Lanka Robert Blake emphasized US concern about the plight of the civilians trapped in the 'civilian safe zone' in northern Sri Lanka. They called on the LTTE to release the civilians and reiterated that both the LTTE and the Sri Lankan government should stop firing into and from the no fire zone. They also emphasized the urgent need for the government and the LTTE, including Diaspora communities around the world, to find a political end of the conflict.
[*Assistant Secretary Boucher and Ambassador Blake discuss humanitarian situation in Sri Lanka with Tamil Diaspora groups*, Bureau of Public Affairs, US Department of State, 8 April 2009 -
www.state.gov/r/pa/prs/ps/2009/04/121487.htm]

Artillery shells hit at 7.30am near the Pokkanai primary health centre inside the 'civilian safe zone', where hundreds of civilians were waiting in line to receive food, killing at least 13 civilians and wounding over 50 others. The doctor who examined the site two hours after the attack said that the shells were 120mm rounds and appeared to have been fired from Sri Lanka army positions south of the safe zone.
[*Sri Lanka: Stop Shelling 'No-Fire Zone'*, Human Rights Watch, 9 April 2009 -
www.hrw.org/en/news/2009/04/09/sri-lanka-stop-shelling-no-fire-zone]

A doctor at the Puthumathalan makeshift hospital in Mullaitivu District said the hospital received 296 wounded and 46 bodies from Pokkanai within the 'civilian safe zone'.
[*Sri Lanka: Stop Shelling 'No-Fire Zone'*, Human Rights Watch, 9 April 2009 -
www.hrw.org/en/news/2009/04/09/sri-lanka-stop-shelling-no-fire-zone]

9 April
The Sri Lanka army shelled the makeshift Puthumathalan hospital and the Puthumathalan Mother and Child Centre in Mullaitivu District, killing 22 people.
[*Sri Lanka Repeated shelling of hospitals evidence of war crimes*, Human Rights Watch, 8 May 2009 -
www.hrw.org/en/news/2009/05/08/sri-lanka-repeated-shelling-hospitals-evidence-war-crimes]

April 2009

The Puthumathalan makeshift hospital in Mullaitivu District received 300 wounded persons and 62 bodies, according to the doctors. Forty seven of the injured victims died after admission to the hospital.

[*Sri Lanka: Stop Shelling 'No-Fire Zone'*, Human Rights Watch, 9 April 2009 www.hrw.org/en/news/2009/04/09/sri-lanka-stop-shelling-no-fire-zone; [*Carnage continues in Vanni*, TamilNet, 9 April 2009 - www.tamilnet.com/art.html?catid=13&artid=28991]

The ICRC evacuated 230 injured civilians and their relatives by ferry from Puthumathalan in Mullaitivu District to Trincomalee.

[*Sri Lanka: Stop Shelling 'No-Fire Zone'*, Human Rights Watch, 9 April 2009 - www.hrw.org/en/news/2009/04/09/sri-lanka-stop-shelling-no-fire-zone]

Human Rights Watch (HRW) said that the Sri Lankan government should stop firing heavy artillery into the 'civilian safe zone' in the northern Vanni area where some 100,000 civilians were trapped, causing skyrocketing casualties. HRW called upon the UN Security Council to take urgent measures, including by sending a special envoy to Sri Lanka, to bring an end to violations of international humanitarian law by government forces and the LTTE.

[*Sri Lanka: Stop Shelling 'No-Fire Zone'*, Human Rights Watch, 9 April 2009 www.hrw.org/en/news/2009/04/09/sri-lanka-stop-shelling-no-fire-zone]

10 April

Seventy two Tamil civilians were killed in Sri Lanka army attacks at Valaiyanmadam and Pokkanai areas in Mullaitivu District.

[*SLA build-up poses severe threat to civilian security within 'safety zone'*, TamilNet, 11 April 2009 - www.tamilnet.com/art.html?catid=13&artid=29010

11 April

Seventeen Tamil civilians were killed and 48 others were injured in Sri Lanka army attacks on the 'civilian safe zone' in Mullaitivu District.

[*SLA embarks upon capturing attack on civilians, 300 shells explode within 45 minutes*, TamilNet, 11 April 2009 www.tamilnet.com/art.html?catid=13&artid=29016]

12 April

Sri Lanka army attacks on the 'civilian safe zone' in Mullaitivu District killed 31 Tamil civilians and wounded at least 36 others.

[*31 civilians killed in SLA shelling, gunfire in 'safety zone'*, TamilNet, 12 April 2009 www.tamilnet.com/art.html?catid=13&artid=29022]

The Sri Lankan government declared a two-day ceasefire to allow emergency humanitarian aid to reach thousands of civilians caught up in the conflict in the Vanni.

[*Sri Lanka civilians stay in war zone despite lull*, Associated Press, 13 April 2009 www3.signonsandiego.com/stories/2009/apr/13/sri-lanka-civil-war-041309/

13 April

Sri Lanka army shells and gunfire killed at least 23 Tamil civilians. Most of the civilian casualties were reported in Valaiyanmadam and Mullivaikal within the 'civilian safe zone' in Mullaitivu District.

April 2009

[*SLA attacks kill 23 Tamil civilians within 12 hours*, TamilNet, 13 April 2009
www.tamilnet.com/art.html?catid=13&artid=29030]

The President of the UN General Assembly Miguel d'Escoto Brockmann welcomed the ceasefire declared by Sri Lanka on 12 April 2009, but expressed concern over the humanitarian disaster faced by the people. He noted the lack of adequate food, water and sanitary conditions arising from military operations as well as aerial bombings that have injured many civilians.
[*GA President calls for permanent ceasefire in Sri Lanka*, Statement of the Spokesperson of the President of the UN General Assembly, 13 April 2009   www.un.org/ga/president/63/news/pressrelease130409.pdf]

14 April
Forty three Tamil civilians injured by Sri Lanka army attacks on the 'civilian safe zone' were admitted to the makeshift hospital at Puthumathalan in Mullaitivu District.
[*SLA continues offensive at the doorstep of 'safe zone'*, TamilNet, 14 April 2009
www.tamilnet.com/art.html?catid=13&artid=29039]

15 April
At least 180 Tamil civilians were feared killed between Mullivaikal to Pokkanai when the Sri Lanka army launched heavy attacks on the 'civilian safe zone'. Civilians struggled to transport the wounded to the hospital. The makeshift hospital at Puthumathalan received 83 wounded civilians and six died on admission.
[*Unprecedented carnage, SLA turns firepower on civilian zone*, TamilNet, 15 April 2009
www.tamilnet.com/art.html?catid=13&artid=29048; *SLA offensive on civilian zone continues*, TamilNet, 15 April 2009 - www.tamilnet.com/art.html?catid=13&artid=29051]

16 April
More than 57 Tamil civilians were killed in Mullivaikal and Iraddaivaikal and Pokkanai areas in Mullaitivu District. The Puthumathalan makeshift hospital received 130 injured civilians, seven of whom died after admission.
[*Onslaught of civilians continues, more than 57 killed, 300 wounded Thursday*, TamilNet, 16 April 2009 - www.tamilnet.com/art.html?catid=13&artid=29064]

17 April
UN Secretary-General's Chief of Staff, Vijay Nambiar arrived in Sri Lanka for a two day official visit. He met President Mahinda Rajapaksa, Defence Secretary Gotabaya Rajapaksa and other officials. Among the key issues discussed was how the UN could assist people leaving the 'civilian safe zone' in Mullaitivu District.
[Update Report No. 5 Sri Lanka, UN Security Council, 21 April 2009 –
www.securitycouncilreport.org/site/c.glKWLeMTIsG/b.5113231/k.1322/Update_Report_No_5BRSri_LankaBR21_April_2009.htm]

According to medical authorities at Puthumathalan makeshift hospital, 63 wounded civilians were admitted and two of them died at the hospital.
[*SLA attacks continue to target 'safety zone'*, TamilNet, 19 April 2009 -
www.tamilnet.com/art.html?catid=13&artid=29090]

April 2009

18 April

The Sri Lanka army continued shelling the 'civilian safe zone' targeting Iraddaivaikal, Mullivaikal and Valaiyanmadam. Fifty five wounded civilians, including 30 children, were admitted to the Puthumathalan makeshift hospital. Two of the children died in the hospital.
[*SLA attacks continue to target 'safety zone'*, TamilNet, 19 April 2009
www.tamilnet.com/art.html?catid=13&artid=29090]

20 April

The Sri Lanka army launched heavy attacks in the night killing 13 civilians and injuring hundreds of people at Puthumathalan in Mullaitivu District. Two medical staff at the Puthumathalan makeshift hospital sustained gunshot injuries. The hospital roof and the Surgery Ward were destroyed.
[*Sri Lanka Repeated shelling of hospitals evidence of war crimes*, Human Rights Watch, 8 May 2009 -
www.hrw.org/en/news/2009/05/08/sri-lanka-repeated-shelling-hospitals-evidence-war-crimes]

The Sri Lankan government said that over 58,000 civilians trapped in the 'civilian safe zone' in Mullaitivu District had crossed over into government-controlled territory when the security forces breached a three kilometre-long earthen wall built by the LTTE on the western edge of the zone.
[*58,000 civilians flee no-fire zone*, The Hindu (India), 22 April 2009
www.thehindu.com/2009/04/22/stories/2009042258620100.htm

British Prime Minister Gordon Brown telephoned Sri Lankan President Mahinda Rajapaksa to call for a renewed pause in fighting to allow people to leave the 'civilian safe zone' in Mullaitivu. President Rajapaksa turned down the Prime Minister's request.
[Sri Lanka: Question asked by Baroness Northover, UK House of Lords Hansard, 22 April 2009, Column 1500 - www.publications.parliament.uk/pa/ld200809/ldhansrd/text/90422-0002.htm; *58,000 civilians flee no-fire zone*, The Hindu (India), 22 April 2009 -
www.thehindu.com/2009/04/22/stories/2009042258620100.htm]

The International Crisis Group reported that as many as 150,000 or more civilians were trapped on a strip of land in Mullaitivu District and the area was being shelled by the Sri Lankan military, and the LTTE were using them as human shield hostages. Dozens were dying every day, and there was grave shortage of food, water, and medical treatment.
[*Crisis in Sri Lanka*, International Crisis Group, 20 April 2009
 - www.crisisgroup.org/home/index.cfm?id=6063&l=1]

21 April

Dr. Siva Manoharan and four other medical staff and civilians were killed when the Sri Lanka air force bombed the makeshift hospital in Valaiyanmadam. Thirty others were wounded.
[*SLA cluster bombs kill doctor, medical staff at Valaignarmadam*, TamilNet, 21 April 2009 -
www.tamilnet.com/art.html?catid=13&artid=29112]

The ICRC expressed extreme worry about tens of thousands of civilians, including women, children and elderly people, many of them wounded or sick, trapped in the rapidly shrinking area along the Mullaitivu coast declared a 'civilian safe zone' by the Sri Lankan government. ICRC's Director of Operations, Pierre Krähenbühl said the ongoing fighting has killed or wounded hundreds of civilians who have only minimal access to medical care. Mr. Krähenbühl further said: "The LTTE must keep its

April 2009

fighters and other military resources well away from places where civilians are concentrated, and allow civilians who want to leave the area to do so safely. On their part, government forces are obliged to ensure that the methods and means of warfare they employ make it possible to clearly distinguish at all times between civilians and civilian objects, on the one hand, and military objectives, on the other. In this situation, we are particularly concerned about the impact on civilians of using weapons such as artillery."

[*Sri Lanka: ICRC calls for exceptional precautionary measures to minimize further bloodshed in "no-fire zone"*, ICRC, 21 April 2009   www.icrc.org/Web/Eng/siteeng0.nsf/html/sri-lanka-news-210409]

British aid agency CAFOD's Head of International Programmes, Pauline Taylor-McKeown expressed grave concern at the fate of an estimated 100,000 civilians as the Sri Lankan government announced its intention to conduct a 'final assault' in the Vanni, and a deadline for the LTTE to surrender expired. CAFOD urged the urgent establishment of a 'real' safe zone respected by both sides and monitored by an international third party.

['*Sri Lanka: Final assault' is no answer*, CAFOD, 21 April 2009 www.cafod.org.uk/about-us/what-we-do/emergencies/sri-lanka-2009-04-21]

22 April

Sri Lanka army shells hit Our Lady of Roses Catholic Church in Valaiyanmadam injuring Rev. Fr. James Pathinathan. He was taken by the ICRC to Pulmoddai in Trincomalee District for treatment.

[*SLA shells Church in Valaignarmadam, Fr. James Pathinathar wounded*, TamilNet, 22 April 2009 - www.tamilnet.com/art.html?catid=13&artid=29125]

23 April

Shells fired by the Sri Lanka army at Our Lady of Roses Catholic Church in Valaiyanmadam for the second day in succession killed 14 civilians. Human Development Centre (HUDEC) Director Rev. Fr. T. R. Vasanthaseelan was among the seriously wounded.

[*SLA shelling on church kills 14, Caritas-HUDEC Vanni director wounded*, TamilNet, 23 April 2009 www.tamilnet.com/art.html?catid=13&artid=29135]

24 April

The White House said that Washington was "deeply concerned about the plight of innocent civilians caught up in the conflict" in Sri Lanka. The White House called on Sri Lanka to stop shelling neutral areas and allow international aid groups to work during the nation's civil war.

[Statement on continuing conflict in Sri Lanka, The White House, 25 April 2009 - http://usembassycolombo.blogspot.com/2009/04/white-house-statement-on-situation-in.html]

The *Washington Post* said that according to a private UN document circulated among diplomatic missions in Sri Lanka, at least 6,432 Tamil civilians have been killed in the intense fighting over the past three months and 13,946 wounded. The UN declined to publicly release its casualty figures and had no comment on the document. Civilian deaths increased dramatically, according to the UN. An average of 33 civilians died each day at the end of January 2009, and that figure jumped to 116 by April 2009, the document said. More than 5,500 of those killed were inside the government-declared 'civilian safe zone' on Mullaitivu coast.

April 2009

[*UN says nearly 6,500 civilians killed in Sri Lanka*, The Washington Post, 24 April 2009
www.washingtonpost.com/wp-dyn/content/article/2009/04/24/AR2009042400374.html?hpid=sec-
world]

25 April

As civilians fled the coastal strip in Mullaitivu District to other areas, Trincomalee District Director of
Health Services Dr. E. G. Gnanakunalan said that the displaced people he saw had starved for many
days, were malnourished and needed food. Kilinochchi RDHS Dr. Thangamuthu Sathiyamoorthy said
there was a severe shortage of food and medicines in Kilinochchi and Mullaitivu districts.
[*Trapped Sri Lankans face starvation*, Al Jazeera, 26 April 2009 -
http://english.aljazeera.net/news/asia/2009/04/20094258521937693.html]

Sri Lanka air force planes targeted Mullivaikal in the 'civilian safe zone' in Mullaitivu District. More
than 150 wounded civilians were admitted to the makeshift hospital in Mullivaikal. Fifteen people
died in hospital after admission.
[*Colombo steps up air strikes, safe zone targeted 39 times Sunday*, TamilNet, 26 April 2009
www.tamilnet.com/art.html?catid=13&artid=29172; *Sri Lanka intensifies bombardment, 'safe zone' bombed 25
times Saturday*, TamilNet, 25 April 2009 - www.tamilnet.com/art.html?catid=13&artid=29162]

26 April

A damage assessment by UNITAR/UNOSAT based on a series of high resolution satellite imagery
acquired from 5 February to 19 April 2009 said that within the northern and southern sections of the
'civilian safe zone' (CSZ) in Mullaitivu District, there were new indications of building destruction and
damages resulting from shelling and possible air strikes and that the following figures on building
damages represent minimum estimates as actual damages are likely to be greater:

"**Damages inside CSZ**:

1. **Puttumattalan**: Three permanent buildings have been destroyed between 29 March and 19
   April, bringing the total for the northern section of the CSZ to six destroyed since 15 March.
   There are potentially large amounts of moderate to severe damages to the remaining
   permanent buildings in this area.
2. **Valayanmadam**: 1 additional permanent building has been destroyed, and further south there
   is a cluster of likely impact craters within an area previously densely populated with IDP
   shelters.

"**Damages outside CSZ**:

3. **Puthukkudyiruppu** (PTK): The major concentration of newly detected building destruction and
   hundreds of impact craters is located in the eastern sections of PTK especially centred on the
   main route leading east into the CSZ. This route is now non-functional because of a series of
   road blocks, impact craters and trenches erected along the main road.
4. **Vadduvakallu**: Building destruction continues in Vadduvakallu: 40 buildings destroyed
   between 29 March-19 April 2009 and a total of 148 building destroyed since 5 February 2009.
   A significant number of buildings were destroyed before 5 February 2009.
5. **Mullaitivu**: Building destruction also continues in Mullaitivu with a small number of new
   destruction between 29 March & 19 April.
6. **West of Puthumattalan**: Bridge closed by multiple roadblocks and road damages (29 March-19
   April) (TZ2) transport into CSZ impossible.

April 2009

"IDP (SHELTER) MOVEMENT SUMMARY:
Over five thousand of IDP shelters were relocated within the CSZ during April under pressure from increased shelling and military operations along the western sections of the CSZ. The approximate area of IDP settlement has further shifted eastward towards the coastline and south into the areas of heavy shelling between the villages of Karaiyamullivaikal and Vellamullivaikal.

1. The northern IDP shelter limit has remained stable between 29 March-19 April, however the density of IDPs here has sharply decreased. The southern IDP shelter limit has remained relatively stable between 29 March & 19 April, however the density of IDPs situated in the heavy shelling and damage zone between Karaiyamullivaikal and Vellamullivaikal has increased sharply.

2. Over 5,500 IDP shelters moved from western side of the CSZ (29 March-19 April) likely in response to escalating military activity and shelling. This estimate has been severely limited by cloud and thus is potentially larger by two to four thousand shelters."

[*Updated analysis report (19 April 2009) satellite-detected damages and IDP shelter movement in CSZ, Mullaitivu District, Sri Lanka*, Update 6, UN Operations Satellite Assessment Programme (UNOSAT), UN Institute for Training and Research (UNITAR), 26 April 2009   www.innercitypress.com/UNOSAT19April09.pdf]

Sri Lanka air force attacks in the 'civilian safe zone' caused many deaths and injuries. Fourteen of the 84 people admitted to the makeshift hospital in Mullivaikal died after admission.
[*Colombo steps up air strikes, safe zone targeted 39 times Sunday*, TamilNet, 26 April 2009
www.tamilnet.com/art.html?catid=13&artid=29172]

In a media release, the LTTE announced a unilateral ceasefire with immediate effect, stating that it had taken the decision in the face of an unprecedented humanitarian crisis and in response to the calls made by the UN, EU, the governments of the USA, India and others. The LTTE said that all of its offensive military operations will cease with immediate effect, and called on the international community to pressure the Sri Lankan government to reciprocate the ceasefire. Sri Lanka's Defence Secretary Gotabaya Rajapaksa dismissed the announcement as "a joke" and insisted that the LTTE must surrender.
[*Announcement of unilateral ceasefire by LTTE*, The Hindu (India), 26 April 2009
www.hindu.com/nic/ceasefire.htm; *Sri Lanka rebels call ceasefire*, BBC, 26 April 2009
http://news.bbc.co.uk/1/hi/8019199.stm]

27 April
The Council of the European Union urged the Sri Lanka government to cooperate fully with the mission of the UN Under-Secretary-General for Humanitarian Affairs John Holmes, to release UN staff members detained in IDP camps and to allow international oversight of all IDPs as soon as they have left the conflict zone. The Council called on Sri Lanka to fulfil the commitments it had made to improve the condition in the IDP camps including: better access to medical facilities; transparent registration processes; international monitoring; and freedom of movement in and out of the camps.
[*Council conclusions on Sri Lanka*, 2939th External Relations Council meeting, Luxembourg, 27 April 2009, Council of the European Union   www.dellka.ec.europa.eu/en/whatsnew/2009/pdf/PR-GAERC_090427.pdf]

April 2009

The Sri Lanka air force and the navy targeted the 'civilian safe zone', particularly Valaiyanmadam, Mullivaikal and Vadduvakal. One hundred and thirty nine injured civilians were admitted to the hospital and 19 of them died after admission.

[*Sri Lanka steps up intense barrage of heavy weapons*, TamilNet, 27 April 2009 - www.tamilnet.com/art.html?catid=13&artid=29201]

Sri Lanka military spokesman Brigadier Udaya Nanayakkara said that the army were using small arms in the fighting against the LTTE and were not using heavy weapons.

[*Sri Lanka says combat gives way to rescue*, Reuters, 27 April 2009 - www.reuters.com/article/homepageCrisis/idUSCOL398804._CH_.2400]

The Sri Lankan government announced that it was ending the use of air and artillery strikes in its war with the LTTE, after weeks of denying that it was using such weapons. "Our security forces have been instructed to end the use of heavy calibre guns, combat aircraft and aerial weapons which could cause civilian casualties," the government said. The statement appeared to contradict previous claims by the military that it had not been using heavy weapons.

[*Sri Lanka army to end air strikes on Tamil Tigers*, The Guardian (UK), 27 April 2009 - www.guardian.co.uk/world/2009/apr/27/sri-lanka-tamil-tigers]

RDHS Dr. Thangamutha Sathiyamoorthy, working in the 'civilian safe zone' in Mullaitivu District reported that there were nine air strikes on Mullivaikal south area on 27 April. He said 154 civilians were admitted to the temporary hospital at Mullivaikal on 25 April 2009 with injuries sustained in air strikes, shelling and attacks by gun boats, and 15 victims died. He said another 84 were admitted on 26 April 2009 and 14 had died. The Sri Lanka government accused Dr. Sathiyamoorthy of acting as a mouthpiece for the LTTE.

[*Sri Lanka army to end air strikes on Tamil Tigers*, The Guardian (UK), 27 April 2009 - www.guardian.co.uk/world/2009/apr/27/sri-lanka-tamil-tigers]

28 April

Six previously injured patients receiving treatment in the Mullivaikal Primary Health Centre in the 'civilian safe zone' in Mullaitivu District were killed in Sri Lanka army and the air force attacks. A member of the medical staff was injured.

[*Sri Lanka Repeated shelling of hospitals evidence of war crimes*, Human Rights Watch, 8 May 2009 www.hrw.org/en/news/2009/05/08/sri-lanka-repeated-shelling-hospitals-evidence-war-crimes]

In a meeting with President Mahinda Rajapaksa after visiting IDP camps in northern Sri Lanka, UN Under-Secretary-General for Humanitarian Affairs John Holmes reiterated concerns over the level of civilian casualties, and the urgent need to assist the tens of thousands of civilians still trapped in the conflict zone, particularly with food aid and medical supplies. He said Sri Lanka faced two distinct crises: First, there were tens of thousands of people trapped on a small patch of territory in the north, with the LTTE refusing to let them leave, and with fighting continuing; second, the swollen camps that were filling up with 200,000 people who fled the fighting, many in very poor condition, with more likely on the way soon.

[*UN concern about Sri Lanka's twin humanitarian crises*, UN News Centre, 28 April 2009 www.reliefweb.int/rw/rwb.nsf/db900SID/JBRN-7RJDRX?OpenDocument]

April 2009

29 April

British Foreign Secretary David Miliband and French Foreign Minister Bernard Kouchner called on the Sri Lankan President Mahinda Rajapakse to urge the government to declare an immediate ceasefire and give civilians trapped in the country's war zone a chance to escape.
[*Miliband urges Sri Lanka to call truce with Tamil Tigers*, The Guardian (UK), 29 April 2009 www.guardian.co.uk/world/2009/apr/29/miliband-sri-lanka-tamil-tigers]

The Sri Lanka navy fired on Mullivaikal makeshift hospital in the 'civilian safe zone' in Mullaitivu District killing nine patients and injuring 15 others. More than 150 other dead bodies of civilians were recovered in the Mullivaikal area.
[*Hospital attacked, SLN naval crafts fire artillery pieces*, TamilNet, 29 April 2009 www.tamilnet.com/art.html?catid=13&artid=29215]

A shell fired by the Sri Lanka army hit the Mullivaikal Primary Health Centre in Mullaitivu District, killing six patients.
[*Sri Lanka Repeated shelling of hospitals evidence of war crimes, Human Rights Watch*, 8 May 2009 - www.hrw.org/en/news/2009/05/08/sri-lanka-repeated-shelling-hospitals-evidence-war-crimes]

30 April

With the number of people crossing out of the conflict zone in northern Sri Lanka growing daily, and several camps in and around Vavuniya already very congested, Spokesperson for the UN Secretary General, Marie Okabe voiced UN's continuing concern at a press conference in New York, over accommodations for civilians fleeing the fighting, and urged the government to make available all public buildings and usable land for the accommodation of the large number of civilians. The UN Office for the Coordination of Humanitarian Affairs (UN OCHA) said some 172,000 people had crossed out of the conflict zone in the Vanni.
[*Housing for growing Sri Lanka's displaced major concern*, UN News Centre, 30 April 2009 - www.un.org/apps/news/story.asp?NewsID=30654&Cr=sri+lanka&Cr1=&Kw1=Sri+Lanka&Kw2=&Kw3=]

May 2009

1 May

In an interview to Al Jazeera, Foreign Secretary Palitha Kohona admitted that Sri Lankan forces had targeted a number of rebel positions inside the 'civilian safe zone' in retaliation for LTTE's artillery fire, but denied any civilians were in the area at the time of the raid. The admission came after satellite pictures showed evidence of aerial bombing of the zone between 5 February and 19 April shortly after the government declared it a 'civilian safe zone'. Mr Kohona said: "As long as the retaliation is proportionate, it is perfectly legitimate and what we did exactly was locate these guns and retaliate against those guns. But I would challenge anybody to say that these shell holes were created once the civilians moved into the area and it became occupied by civilians." But on 19 April 2009, Mr. Kohona had said that there was no government shelling in the 'civilian safe zone' and that the government had issued very strict instructions to the military not to use aerial bombing or shelling into the zone.

[*Sri Lanka admits bombing safe zone*, Al Jazeera, 2 May 2009
http://english.aljazeera.net/news/asia/2009/05/20095141557222873.html; *Sri Lanka government admits bombing civilian safe haven*, The Times (UK), 1 May 2009 -
www.timesonline.co.uk/tol/news/world/asia/article6206708.ece]

According to doctors working in Mullaitivu, 27 civilians were killed in Sri Lanka army artillery fire in Mullivaikal within the 'civilian safe zone'. The hospital at Mullivaikal received 110 wounded civilians and 27 of them died in the hospital.

[*Hospital 'hit by Sri Lankan army'*, BBC 2 May 2009 -
http://news.bbc.co.uk/1/hi/world/south_asia/8030605.stm; *SLA steps up attacks, civilian casualties mount amidst starvation*, congested life, TamilNet, 1 May 2009 -
www.tamilnet.com/art.html?catid=13&artid=29237]

President of the International Crisis Group Gareth Evans said that both the LTTE leadership and the Sri Lankan government have abdicated their responsibility to protect civilians from mass-atrocity crimes. In an article he criticized UN's failure to protect civilians in Sri Lanka:

"And the tragedy is that they have now been joined in this abdication by the Security Council itself, notwithstanding the unanimous resolution of the General Assembly, meeting at the heads of government level in 2005, that it should take "timely and decisive" action when "national authorities are failing to protect their populations from genocide, war crimes, ethnic cleansing and crimes against humanity". To their credit, France, the United States, Britain, and a number of other proactive Security Council members have ratcheted up pressure in recent weeks. They have pushed - albeit cautiously - for the council to review Sri Lanka as an official agenda item, and carefully negotiated a series of informal remarks on behalf of the council.

"But because of consistent obstruction by a handful of member states, the issue continues to be relegated to informal statements and unofficial meetings - not in the Security Council chamber - but in the basement of the U.N. building. Those signalling varying degrees of opposition to council engagement have been China, Russia, Libya, Vietnam and - most surprisingly and disappointingly, given its role in advocating human security generally and civilian protection specifically - Japan. While the tacit approval of a military endgame against a terrorist group is understandable enough,

May 2009

looking the other way as tens of thousands of innocent civilians are imperilled in the process is indefensible.

"Well aware of the absence of determined and united international action - by the council in particular - the government has defaulted on its promises and paid mere lip service to calls for restraint, all the while pursuing its military onslaught. But Colombo's intense efforts to prevent a review by the Security Council, with much lobbying in member state capitals, show how much weight effective council action would have.

"It must be made crystal clear to both the Tigers and the Sri Lankan government that they will be held accountable for their actions. The council could consider a U.N. commission of inquiry to examine the likelihood of war crimes committed by both sides."
[*Sri Lanka: "Falling down on the Job"*, International Crisis Group, 1 May 2009
www.crisisgroup.org/home/index.cfm?id=6086]

2 May

The Sri Lanka army fired artillery shells twice on the makeshift hospital at Mullivaikal in Mullaitivu District killing 64 patients and relatives, and causing injuries to 87 others. The attack took place even though the military had been provided the coordinates of the hospital by the ICRC. Those killed included a woman volunteer doctor. Three medical staff were among the wounded. The hospital was relocated to the Mullivaikal Junior School.
[*SLA massacres patients with targeted shelling, 64 killed in hospital,* TamilNet, 2 May 2009
www.tamilnet.com/art.html?catid=13&artid=29240]

3 May

Sri Lanka army attacks on the 'civilian safe zone' in Mullaitivu District killed or injured many civilians. The makeshift hospital at Mullivaikal received 814 wounded persons, including 112 children. The hospital also received 257 dead bodies, including 67 of children, have been brought to the hospital.
[2,000 civilians feared slaughtered in a single night, TamilNet, 10 May 2009
www.tamilnet.com/art.html?catid=13&artid=29311]

5 May

UK's Channel 4 TV News reported that shocking claims have emerged from IDP camps in Vavuniya of shortages of food and water, dead bodies left where they have fallen, women separated from their families, and even sexual abuse. At least 100,000 Tamils from the country's north were held in these camps, and while the Sri Lankan government insisted their stay was temporary, aid workers said there is no concrete plan for their resettlement. People in the camps gave the first independent testimony of life inside: Stories of children trampled in the rush to get food; of three women's bodies found in a bathing area in the open. The information emerged at a time when the camps are the subject of great controversy. According to Channel 4, the international community, through the UN and aid agencies, are helping to build and organize aid inside the growing camp network which may one day need to hold 230,000 people. Critics said the UN money is in effect being used to help the Sri Lankan government build a huge internment camp system.

May 2009

[*Grim scenes at Sri Lankan camps*, Channel 4 TV (UK), 5 May 2009
www.channel4.com/news/articles/politics/international_politics/grim+scenes+at+sri+lankan+camps+
/3126257]

7 May

The ICRC evacuated 495 sick and injured patients and accompanying caregivers from Mullaitivu. ICRC's head of operations for South Asia Jacques de Maio said that heavy fighting near the medical assembly point at Mullivaikkal put the lives of patients, medical workers and ICRC staff at great risk and hampered medical evacuations of wounded civilians and their families. For seven days prior to this operation, security constraints had prevented the ICRC from rescuing dozens of patients in need of urgent medical treatment. The ICRC said that since 10 February, it had evacuated more than 13,000 people from the conflict area by boat to government-controlled Trincomalee and Pulmoddai.
[*Sri Lanka: ICRC evacuates 495 from conflict zone and delivers 25 tonnes of food*, ICRC, 7 May 2009 -
www.icrc.org/web/eng/siteeng0.nsf/htmlall/sri-lanka-news-070509?opendocument]

Sri Lankan President Mahinda Rajapaksa appointed a 19-member Presidential Task Force for Resettlement, Development and Security in the Northern Province headed by Presidential Advisor Basil Rajapaksa, with Essential Services Commissioner General S. B. Divarathne as Secretary. The Task Force was mandated to prepare strategic plans, programmes and projects to resettle IDPs, rehabilitate and develop economic and social infrastructure of the Northern Province, to be completed within one year. The Task Force was also asked to carry out the following tasks: (1) coordinate activities of government security agencies in support of resettlement, rehabilitation and development; (2) direct and oversee implementation of plans and programmes of the relevant state organizations and provincial authorities; (3) liaise with organizations in the public and private sectors and civil society for proper implementation; (4) find innovative solutions to problems and constraints in the execution of the mandate of the Task Force; (5) regularly review the progress of the implementation and take corrective actions.

Other members of the Task Force: Presidential Secretary Lalith Weeratunge; Defence Secretary Gotabaya Rajapaksa; Finance and Planning Secretary Sumith Abeysinghe; Resettlement and Disaster Relief Services Secretary U. L. M. Haldeen; Nation Building and Estate Infrastructure Development Secretary W. K. K. Kumarasiri; Highways and Road Development Secretary S.Amarasekera; Power and Energy Secretary M. M. C. Ferdinando; Land and Land Development Secretary J. R. W. Dissanayake; Health Care and Nutrition Secretary Dr. Athula Kahandaliyanage; Chief of Defence Staff Air Chief Marshal G. D. Perera; Army Commander Lt. Gen. Sarath Fonseka; Navy Commander Vice Admiral Wasantha Karannagoda; Air Force Commander Air Marshall W. D. R. M. J. Gunatillake; Inspector General of Police Jayantha Wickremarathne; Director General of Civil Defence Rear Admiral S. P. Weerasekera; Competent Authority for the Northern Province Maj. Gen. G. A. Chandrasiri; Former Director General National Planning B.Abeygunewardena.
[*Presidential Task Force on Northern Development*, Sri Lanka Ministry of Foreign Affairs, 7 May 2009
www.slmfa.gov.lk/index.php?option=com_content&task=view&id=1730&Itemid=1]

8 May

Human Rights Watch said the Sri Lankan armed forces have repeatedly struck hospitals in the northern Vanni region in indiscriminate artillery and aerial attacks and commanders responsible for

May 2009

ordering or conducting such attacks may be prosecuted for war crimes. Patients, medical staff, aid workers, and other witnesses have provided information about at least 30 attacks on permanent and makeshift hospitals in the combat area since December 2008. Brad Adams, Asia director at Human Rights Watch said: "Hospitals are supposed to be sanctuaries from shelling, not targets. While doctors and nurses struggle to save lives in overcrowded and underequipped facilities, Sri Lankan army attacks have hit one hospital after another."

[*Sri Lanka: Repeated shelling of hospitals evidence of war crimes: 30 attacks reported on medical facilities since December May 8*, 2009 - www.hrw.org/en/news/2009/05/08/sri-lanka-repeated-shelling-hospitals-evidence-war-crimes]

UN Human Rights Council experts Philip Alston, Anand Grover, Olivier De Schutter and Catarina de Albuquerque, dealing with (1) summary executions, (2) right to health, (3) right to food and (4) water and sanitation, expressed deep concern in a statement in Geneva over the humanitarian crisis in Sri Lanka, not only in terms of the civilians who have been and continue to be killed, but because of a dramatic lack of transparency and accountability. They said that there was good reason to believe that thousands of civilians have been killed in the past three months alone, and yet the Sri Lankan government has yet to account for the casualties, or to provide access to the war zone for journalists and humanitarian monitors of any type.

"The civilians did not have sufficient access to food, essential medical supplies or services and safe water and sanitation. Even if they escaped death or injury at the hands of the hostile parties, their continued presence in the area without access to these basic rights was an effective death sentence. Shipments of food and medicine to the "no fire zone" have been grossly insufficient over the past month and the government has reportedly delayed or denied timely shipment of life saving medicines as well as to chlorine tablets.

"Civilians escaping the zone continue to face scant supplies, entirely insufficient access to adequate medical treatment and severely overcrowded hospitals, providing no relief to the horrors they had been living. Access to food has also been hampered by arduous and lengthy registration procedures for the IDPs; water shortages were reported at Omanthai and at most of the transit sites as well as inadequate sanitation facilities, which put the health and lives of the population at further risk."

The Experts called upon the Sri Lankan government to provide convincing evidence to the international community that it is respecting its obligations under human rights and international humanitarian law. They said it was also clear that the LTTE has acted in flagrant violation of the applicable norms by preventing civilians from leaving the conflict area and having reportedly shot and killed those trying to flee. The Experts called upon the UN Human Rights Council to urgently establish an international commission of inquiry to study the conduct of all sides to the conflict, to document the events of recent months and to monitor ongoing developments.

[*Urgent international scrutiny needed in Sri Lanka, say UN Human Rights Experts*, UN Press Release, 8 May 2009 www.unhchr.ch/huricane/huricane.nsf/view01/57D5CC3A9B1271B2C12575B000492130?opendocument]

Sri Lanka army headquarters announced that the 'civilian safe zone' had been reduced from 20 sq. km. to 3 sq. km. after considering the concentration of civilians in the area. The safe zone was

May 2009

restricted to a strip, south of Karaiyamullivaikkal including Vellamullivaikkal, with an area of some 2 km in length and 1.5 km in width (Annex 3).

[*No fire zone area reduced: military*, Sri Lanka Guardian, 8 May 2009
www.srilankaguardian.org/2009/05/no-fire-zone-area-reduced-military.html]

10 May

Asia correspondent of UK Channel 4 News Nick Paton Walsh, cameraman Matt Jasper and producer Bessie Du were deported from Sri Lanka for exposing Vavuniya IDP camp conditions in a report on 5 May 2009. They had been arrested in Trincomalee on 9 May. Lakshman Hulugalle, the head of the government Security Information Centre, said the journalists admitted they had "done something wrong" and would not be allowed to come back to Sri Lanka. Nick Paton Walsh denied giving a statement to police or admitting wrongdoing. He said that on 8 May he received a telephone call from the Sri Lankan Defence Secretary, Gotabaya Rajapaksa, who said: "You have been accusing my soldiers of raping civilians? Your visa is cancelled, you will be deported. You can report what you like about this country, but from your own country, not from here."

Channel 4 referred to Amnesty International's report that at least 14 local journalists and Sri Lankans working for media organisations have been killed since the beginning of 2006. Others have been detained, tortured or have disappeared and 20 more have fled the country because of death threats.

[*Sri Lanka throws out three Channel 4 journalists*, Channel 4 TV (UK), 10 May 2009
www.guardian.co.uk/world/2009/may/10/channel-four-journalists-sri-lanka; *Journalist who reported on internment camps in Sri Lanka tells his story*, The Guardian (UK), 10 May 2009
www.guardian.co.uk/world/2009/may/10/channel-4-sri-lanka]

11 May

After heavy shelling of the 'civilian safe zone' by Sri Lankan government forces on 9 and 10 May 2009, government doctor V. Shanmugarajah, working at a makeshift hospital within the zone, said that 430 civilians, including 106 children, had been brought for burial or died at the facility and that a male nurse and his family had died when the trench in which they were sheltering caved in. He estimated more than 1,300 wounded civilians had been brought to the hospital for treatment. Many of the dead were buried in mass graves near the hospital.

[*Sri Lankan government defends army massacre*, Centre for Research and Globalization, 12 May 2009
www.globalresearch.ca/index.php?context=va&aid=13591]

Sri Lanka Defence Secretary Gotabaya Rajapaksa dismissed civilian deaths in Mullaitivu as an LTTE "propaganda lie" timed to coincide with an informal UN Security Council session and to "force the international community to stop the offensive". He said "nothing could be as ridiculous as a claim of over 2,000 civilians being killed in a single barrage".

[*Spin docs create casualty figures to mislead UN - Secretary Defence*, Sri Lanka Defence Ministry, 11 May 2009 -
www.defence.lk/new.asp?fname=20090511_03]

UN spokesman in Colombo, Gordon Weiss, branded the attacks on people in the Mullaitivu 'civilian safe zone' a bloodbath. "The UN has consistently warned against the bloodbath scenario as we've watched the steady increase in civilian deaths over the last few months. The large-scale killing of civilians over the weekend, including the deaths of more than 100 children, shows that the

May 2009

bloodbath has become a reality," he said. Pointing to the large number of injured, Mr. Weiss warned: "Many of those civilians may die in the coming days because we cannot reach them with medical care."

[*Sri Lankan government defends army massacre*, Centre for Research on Globalization, 12 May 2009 - www.globalresearch.ca/index.php?context=va&aid=13591

British Foreign Secretary David Miliband co-hosted a meeting at the Security Council on the crisis in Sri Lanka. The gathering was not technically a meeting of the Security Council because Russia and China opposed any formal Council discussions on the issue, claiming it is a matter internal to Sri Lanka.

[*Sri Lanka at the Security Council--Or Not*, UN Dispatch, 12 May 2009 - www.undispatch.com/node/8220]

12 May

In a joint statement in Washington, US Secretary of State, Hillary Clinton and British Foreign Secretary, David Miliband expressed alarm at the large number of reported civilian causalities in the designated 'civilian safe zone' in northern Sri Lanka and called on the government to abide by its commitment of 27 April 2009 to end major combat operations and the use of heavy weapons, and the LTTE to lay down arms and allow civilians free passage out of the conflict zone. They expressed their appreciation for the efforts of the UN and their staff in Sri Lanka and urged the government and the LTTE to allow a UN humanitarian team to visit the conflict zone to facilitate the safe evacuation of civilians. They called for a political solution that reconciles all Sri Lankans, and establishes a meaningful role for Tamil and other minorities in national political life.

[*Joint US/UK statement on the humanitarian situation in Sri Lanka*, Foreign and Commonwealth Office (UK), 12 May 2009 - www.fco.gov.uk/en/newsroom/latest-news/?view=PressS&id=17650013]

Forty five people were killed when the Sri Lanka army carried out a bomb attack on the makeshift Mullivaikal hospital inside the official 'civilian safe zone' in Mullaitivu District. Dr Thurairaja Varatharajah, the senior government health official in the war zone, said that about 50 people were wounded in the attack and the death toll could rise.

[*Sri Lanka accused of 'war crime' over shelled hospital*, The Daily Telegraph (UK), 12 May 2009 www.telegraph.co.uk/news/worldnews/asia/srilanka/5313308/Sri-Lanka-accused-of-war-crime-over-shelled-hospital.html]

Amnesty International demanded the UN Security Council to convene without delay and take immediate action regarding the horrific condition facing civilians in north eastern Sri Lanka which has been described as a "bloodbath" by the UN. "The controversy over who is responsible for these devastating attacks underlines the need for the Security Council to demand immediate access to the area by humanitarian organizations as well as UN observers. The Security Council should emphasise that both the government and the LTTE will be held fully accountable for any breaches of their obligations under international humanitarian and human rights law," said Sam Zarifi, Amnesty International's Asia-Pacific Director. In its letter to Security Council members, Amnesty also urged the appointment of a Commission of Inquiry to investigate violations of international law.

[*Sri Lanka: Security Council must act*, Amnesty International, 12 May 2009 www.amnesty.org.au/news/comments/20961/]

May 2009

13 May

After a visit of a Vice Ministerial Troika from the EU to Sri Lanka on 12 and 13 May 2009, the EU expressed deep concern about the high number of civilian casualties and deteriorating humanitarian situation in northern Sri Lanka and reiterated its primary concern for the civilians in the conflict zone who were surviving under appalling conditions. The EU also raised concern about lack of access to the screening points and conditions in the holding centres for IDPs and reiterated the importance of the Sri Lanka government facilitating humanitarian access to civilians in need.
[*EU Troika visit to Sri Lanka*, Council of the European Union, 12-13 May 2009
www.dellka.ec.europa.eu/en/whatsnew/2009/pdf/PR-09-05-13_Troika.pdf

Following a meeting of eight members of the Security Council with UN officials and humanitarian NGOs on 12 May 2009, the members of the Council expressed grave concern over the worsening humanitarian crisis in north-east Sri Lanka, in particular the reports of hundreds of civilian casualties in recent days, and called for urgent action by all parties to ensure the safety of civilians. They strongly condemned the LTTE for its continued use of civilians as human shields and demanded that the LTTE lay down its arms and allow civilians in the conflict zone to leave. They also expressed deep concern at the reports of continued use of heavy calibre weapons in areas with high concentrations of civilians, and expected the Sri Lanka government to fulfil its commitment in this regard. They called on the government to take the further necessary steps to facilitate the evacuation of the trapped civilians and the urgent delivery of humanitarian assistance to them.
[*Security Council press statement on Sri Lanka*, Security Council, SC/9659, 13 May 2009
http://huwu.org/News/Press/docs/2009/sc9659.doc.htm]

14 May

UK Foreign and Commonwealth Minister Bill Rammell indicated in the British House of Commons that some members of the UN Security Council were opposed to a resolution on Sri Lanka. Edward Davey, MP for Kingston and Surbiton said that he examined the matter and found that it is the Chinese who are the real block in the Security Council, although they were hiding behind the Russians earlier. Mr. Davey also said that the Chinese have a massive vested interest because China is now the biggest donor of aid to Sri Lanka, and while India and western governments have refused to sell weapons to the Colombo government, it has been the Chinese who have been supplying those weapons. He urged the British government to exercise influence, and request the US government to exercise its influence, on the Chinese government.
 [House of Commons Debates (UK), Hansard for 14 May 2009, Columns 1034-1058
www.parliament.the-stationery-office.co.uk/pa/cm200809/cmhansrd/cm090514/debtext/90514-0006.htm]

15 May

ICRC Operations Director Pierre Krahenbuhl said fighting in Mullaitivu forced the ICRC to temporarily halt evacuations and aid to those trapped on the northeast coast. He added that ICRC staff witnessed "an unimaginable humanitarian catastrophe", and that people were left to their own devices without humanitarian help.
[*Fighting rages in Sri Lanka, more civilians flee*, Reuters, 15 May 2009   www.hcfa.com/?p=5980]

May 2009

17 May

Sri Lankan Human Rights Minister Mahinda Samarasinghe claimed that soldiers saved all Tamil civilians trapped inside the war zone in the Vanni without shedding a drop of blood.

[*Times photographs expose Sri Lanka's lie on civilian deaths at beach*, The Times (UK), May 29, 2009 www.timesonline.co.uk/tol/news/world/asia/article6383477.ece]

19 May

Sri Lanka army commander General Sarath Fonseka disclosed that the body of LTTE leader Velupillai Prabhakaran has been found near the Nanthikadal lagoon in Mullaitivu District by soldiers of the 53rd Division of the army. Military spokesman Udaya Nanayakkara said that the LTTE leader had died due to gunshot injury to his head.

[*Prabhakaran's body found Army Chief*, Daily News, 20 May 2009 www.dailynews.lk/2009/05/20/sec01.asp]

Addressing the ceremonial opening of the Sri Lanka Parliament, President Mahinda Rajapaksa announced that the LTTE had been defeated in the 25-year civil war. He claimed that the defeat of the LTTE and the breakdown of their armed strength will never be the defeat of the Tamil people of this country. The President appealed to the expatriates, specially the Tamil people, to return to the island.

[*President's address at the ceremonial opening of parliament*, Daily News (Sri Lanka), 20 May 2009 www.dailynews.lk/2009/05/20/news01.asp]

LTTE's head of International Relations Selvarasa Pathmanathan accused the Sri Lankan government of treachery in the killing of LTTE's political wing leader Balasingham Mahendran (Nadesan) and head of the LTTE Peace Secretariat Seevaratnam Prabhakaran (Pulidevan) when they surrendered to the security forces on 18 May 2009.

[*War crime in the massacre of LTTE officials*, TamilNet, 19 May 2009 - www.tamilnet.com/art.html?catid=13&artid=29409]

In a letter on behalf of 17 nations to the President of the UN Human Rights Council, the Permanent Representative of Germany to the UN Office at Geneva, Reinhard Schweppe, requested convening of a Special Session of the Human Rights Council, entitled "The human rights situation in Sri Lanka" to be held on Monday 25th May 2009. The 17 member nations of the Council were: Argentina, Bosnia and Herzegovina, Canada, Chile, France, Germany, Italy, Mexico, Mauritius, Netherlands, Republic of Korea, Slovakia, Slovenia, Switzerland, Ukraine, the United Kingdom and Uruguay.

[Letter dated 19 May 2009 from the Permanent Representative of Germany to the United Nations Office at Geneva, addressed to the President of the Human Rights Council, Eleventh Special Session 26–27 May 2009, A/HRC/S-11/1, 27 May 2009 http://daccess-dds-ny.un.org/doc/UNDOC/GEN/G09/134/79/PDF/G0913479.pdf?OpenElement]

Foreign Secretary Palitha Kohona said the three doctors taken into custody on 18 May 2009 were under investigation for breaches of the public service regulations which forbid public servants from speaking to the media and revealing confidential information. Doctors Thangamuttu Sathiyamoorthy, Thurairajah Varatharajah and V Shanmugarajah had been staffing makeshift hospitals on a shrinking patch of land in Kilinochchi and Mullaitivu districts. They treated some of the tens of thousands of civilians trapped in the conflict zone as the Sri Lanka army closed in. They reported heavy

May 2009

bombardments and civilian casualties - some in the hospitals in which they were working - that were denied by the government.

[*Appeal to free Sri Lanka doctors*, BBC, 19 May 2009
http://www.bbc.co.uk/sinhala/news/story/2009/05/090519_doctors.shtml]

26 May

UN High Commissioner for Human Rights Navi Pillay said at the opening of the UN Human Rights Council's Special Session on the situation of human rights in Sri Lanka that tens of thousands of civilians had been killed, injured or displaced since December 2008, and accused both sides of grossly disregarding the fundamental principle of the inviolability of civilians. Ms. Pillay urged for an independent and credible international investigation into recent events to ascertain the occurrence, nature and scale of violations of international human rights and humanitarian law, as well as specific responsibilities.

[*Human Rights Council opens eleventh special session on situation of human rights in Sri Lanka*, UN Human Rights Council, 26 May 2009 -
www.unhchr.ch/huricane/huricane.nsf/view01/753D2B41B518DB70C12575C300204176?opendocume nt]

27 May

The Special Session of the Human Rights Council on Sri Lanka concluded after adopting a resolution on assistance to Sri Lanka in the promotion and protection of human rights, in which the Council urged the Sri Lankan government to continue strengthening its activities to ensure that there was no discrimination against ethnic minorities in the enjoyment of the full range of human rights. The Council also commended the measures taken by the government to address the urgent needs of the internally displaced persons. In the resolution, which was adopted by a vote of 29 in favour, 12 against and six abstentions, the Council urged the international community to cooperate with Sri Lanka in the reconstruction efforts, including by increasing the provision of financial assistance, to help the country fight poverty and underdevelopment and continue to ensure the promotion and protection of all human rights, including economic, social and cultural rights. The result of the vote was as follows:

In favour (29): Angola, Azerbaijan, Bahrain, Bangladesh, Bolivia, Brazil, Burkina Faso, Cameroon, China, Cuba, Djibouti, Egypt, Ghana, India, Indonesia, Jordan, Madagascar, Malaysia, Nicaragua, Nigeria, Pakistan, Philippines, Qatar, Russian Federation, Saudi Arabia, Senegal, South Africa, Uruguay, and Zambia.

Against (12): Bosnia and Herzegovina, Canada, Chile, France, Germany, Italy, Mexico, Netherlands, Slovakia, Slovenia, Switzerland, and United Kingdom.

Abstentions (6): Argentina, Gabon, Japan, Mauritius, Republic of Korea, and Ukraine.

[*Report of the Human Rights Council on its eleventh special session*, Human Rights Council, Eleventh special session, 26-27 May 2009, A/HRC/S-11/2
www2.ohchr.org/english/bodies/hrcouncil/docs/11specialsession/A-HRC-S-11-2-E.doc]

Geneva Advocacy Director of Human Rights Watch Juliette de Rivero said the UN Human Rights Council on 27 May 2009 passed a deeply flawed resolution on Sri Lanka that ignores calls for an international investigation into alleged abuses during recent fighting and other pressing human

May 2009

rights concerns. She said that Brazil, Cuba, India and Pakistan led efforts to prevent the passage of a stronger resolution that was put forward by the 17 members of the council that convened the Special Session: Argentina, Bosnia-Herzegovina, Canada, Chile, France, Germany, Italy, Mauritius, Mexico, the Netherlands, Slovenia, Slovakia, South Korea, Switzerland, Ukraine, Uruguay, and the United Kingdom.

"It is deeply disappointing that a majority of the Human Rights Council decided to focus on praising a government whose forces have been responsible for the repeated indiscriminate shelling of civilians. These states blocked a message to the government that it needs to hear, to ensure access to displaced civilians and uphold human rights standards. They undermined the very purpose of the council. A majority of council members - including China, South Africa, and Uruguay - ignored the call for accountability and justice for victims by the UN High Commissioner for Human Rights, Navi Pillay.

"The rejected resolution deplored abuses by both government forces and the LTTE, urged the government to cooperate fully with humanitarian organizations and to provide protection to civilians and displaced persons, and made an appeal to the Sri Lankan government to respect media freedom and investigate attacks against journalists and human rights defenders."
[*Sri Lanka: UN Rights Council fails victims - Member states ignore need for inquiry into wartime violations*, Human Rights Watch, 27 May 2009 - www.hrw.org/en/news/2009/05/27/sri-lanka-un-rights-council-fails-victims]

28 May
French daily *Le Monde* said that the UN deliberately downplayed the number of civilians killed during the Sri Lankan government offensive against the LTTE and that high-ranking UN officials, including Secretary General Ban Ki-moon, chose to keep silent about the high civilian death toll in order to maintain UN operations in the country and avoid slighting the Sri Lankan government. According to *Le Monde*, a group of experts was put together by the UN to compile casualty figures for Sri Lanka, but only a partial total was leaked to the press. UN staff working on the ground informed Vijay Nambiar, UN Secretary General Ban Ki-moon's chief of staff, that the final figures "would without doubt exceed 20,000 dead". Mr Nambiar told UN representatives in Sri Lanka that the UN should "keep a low profile" and play a "sustaining role" that was "compatible with the government". Mr Nambiar's role as the UN's special envoy in Colombo came into question. His brother, Satish Nambiar, a former Indian army general, has been a paid consultant to the Sri Lankan army since 2002. Shortly after the Sri Lankan army's official victory declaration, the Sri Lanka head of UNHCR, Amin Awad, told the Arabic TV station *Al Jazeera* there were virtually no civilians left in the conflict zone. But the next day, some 20,000 refugees came out of the conflict zone, having suffered a sustained bombardment. "It gave the government a blank cheque to carpet bomb the whole area," a UN worker told the *Le Monde*.
[UN *downplayed civilian death toll*, media say, France 24, 29 May 2009 - www.france24.com/en/20090529-un-accused-deliberately-downplaying-civilian-death-toll-sri-lanka-tamil-tigers]

29 May
UK newspaper *The Times* published aerial photographs of the 'civilian safe zone' in Mullaitivu and declared that the UN has no right to collude in suppressing the appalling evidence of atrocities by

May 2009

the Sri Lankan government. The newspaper said that the photographs taken present clear evidence of an atrocity that comes close to matching Srebrenica, Darfur and other massacres.

"In the sandy so-called no-fire zone where the trapped Tamil civilians were told to go to escape the brutal army bombardment, there are hundreds of fresh graves as well as craters and debris where tents once stood. This was no safe zone. This was where terrified civilians buried their dead as the shells landed - after the Government had declared an end to the use of heavy weapons on April 27.

"Finding out what happened, however, is impossible: the army has barred entry to all outsiders. Food is short, sanitation appalling; wounded and traumatised civilians are in desperate need of help. That much is clear from those who have been able to escape. More sinister reports are now circulating of systematic "disappearances", of families separated and young men taken away. But until the Government allows in aid workers, the presumption must be that it wants nothing to be heard or seen of what is going on.

"This tactic was used in the final push to beat the Tigers. The army wanted no witness to the onslaught, no journalists to alert the world to human rights violations, no photographers to record the suffering. Sri Lanka, now basking in its victory, may set the pattern for other nations battling against insurgencies. For them, victory is all that matters. Most of Sri Lanka may rejoice at the end of a bloody civil war. But the UN has no right to collude in suppressing the appalling evidence of the cost. The truth must be told."

[*Slaughter in Sri Lanka*, The Times (UK), 29 May 2009 -
www.timesonline.co.uk/tol/comment/leading_article/article6382706.ece]

UK newspaper *The Times* said that its investigation, including aerial photographs, official documents, witness accounts and expert testimony, has revealed that more than 20,000 Tamil civilians, three times the official figure, were killed in the final throes of the Sri Lankan civil war, most as a result of government shelling in the 'civilian safe zone'.

"Independent defence experts who analysed dozens of aerial photographs taken by *The Times* said that the arrangement of the army and rebel firing positions and the narrowness of the no-fire zone made it unlikely that Tiger mortar fire or artillery caused a significant number of deaths. "It looks more likely that the firing position has been located by the Sri Lankan Army and it has then been targeted with air-burst and ground-impact mortars," said Charles Heyman, editor of the magazine Armed Forces of the UK.

"A spokesman for the Sri Lankan High Commission in London said: "We reject all these allegations. Civilians have not been killed by government shelling at all. If civilians have been killed, then that is because of the actions of the LTTE [rebels] who were shooting and killing people when they tried to escape."

[*The hidden massacre: Sri Lanka's final offensive against Tamil Tigers*, The Times (UK), 29 May 2009
www.timesonline.co.uk/tol/news/world/asia/article6383449.ece]

The ICRC made a public plea for access to the 'civilian safe zone' and internment camps in northern Sri Lanka. Spokesman Florian Westphal said in Geneva that the ICRC has not been able to access the areas where most of these IDPs would have fled from since the ending of the recent fighting.

[*UN chief knew Tamil civilian toll had reached 20,000*, The Times (UK), 30 May 2009
www.timesonline.co.uk/tol/news/world/asia/article6391265.ece]

May 2009

The Sri Lankan government deported Ranvei Tvetenes, the head of Norwegian humanitarian agency FORUT, accusing her of involvement with the LTTE and indulging in activities inimical to the sovereignty and independence of Sri Lanka. Following the fall of the LTTE, she had prevented local Sinhalese staff from celebrating within the FORUT office premises.

[*Norwegian NGO Head Deported*, The Lanka Sun, 31 May 2009
http://lankasun.com:8000/index.php?option=com_content&task=view&id=9062&Itemid=26]

June 2009

1 June

UN Secretary-General Ban Ki-moon denied media reports that the UN covered up a high civilian death toll during the bloody final phase of Sri Lanka's war against the LTTE. Addressing the UN General Assembly, Mr. Ban vehemently rejected the notion that the world body had been involved in a cover-up.

[*Ban denies UN covered up death toll in Sri Lanka*, Reuters, 1 June 2009
www.reuters.com/article/worldNews/idUSTRE5507PG20090601]

2 June

China's Assistant Minister for South Asian Foreign Affairs, Hu Zhengyue said that Sri Lanka should be allowed to tackle its internal affairs and the international community can make concrete efforts to improve the humanitarian condition of the country. He said: "We do not interfere in the internal matters of Sri Lanka as peaceful coexistence, sovereignty and territorial integrity are key ideas in the China's foreign policy on South Asia. However, China will stand by the Sri Lankan Government in its future endeavours in creating peace."

[*Sri Lanka should be allowed to tackle its internal affairs*, Sri Lanka Government, 4 June 2009 -
www.priu.gov.lk/news_update/Current_Affairs/ca200906/20090604sl_should_be_allowed_tackle_internal_affairs.htm]

10 June

Canadian Liberal Member of Parliament, Bob Rae was refused entry into Sri Lanka when he arrived at the Bandaranaike International Airport, due to alleged involvement in pro-LTTE activity in Canada. Mr. Rae is MP for Toronto Centre. Toronto has the largest Sri Lankan expatriate Tamil population in the world.

[*Canadian MP debarred from entry*, Sri Lanka Government, 12 June 2009 -
www.priu.gov.lk/news_update/Current_Affairs/ca200906/20090612canadian_mp_debarred_from_entry.htm]

11 June

Amnesty International said in a report that Commissions of Inquiry in Sri Lanka over a period of twenty years have failed; the formal justice system is in tatters; serious human rights violations (including torture, arbitrary arrest and detention, and violations of the right to life) continue to be committed; and perpetrators continue to be protected by the government. Amnesty called on the international community to stop believing the charade and use its significant influence to encourage the Sri Lankan authorities to investigate past violations, prosecute suspected perpetrators in proceedings which meet international standards of fairness, ensure reparations for victims and prevent future violations.

[*Twenty years of make-believe. Sri Lanka's commissions of inquiry*, Amnesty International, 11 June 2009, ASA 37/005/2009 - www.amnesty.org/en/library/asset/ASA37/005/2009/en/c41db308-7612-4ca7-946d-03ad209aa900/asa370052009eng.pdf]

14 June

The Sri Lankan government announced that the Presidential Commission headed by former Supreme Court justice Nissanka Udalagama, appointed in November 2006 with a mandate to inquire into abductions, disappearances and unexplained killings, has been disbanded.

[*Sri Lanka rights abuse probe ends abruptly*, 16 June 2009

61

June 2009

http://blog.taragana.com/n/sri-lanka-inquiry-into-rights-abuses-ends-with-less-than-half-its-cases-investigated-82744/]

16 June

LTTE's Head of International Relations Selvarasa Pathmanathan announced in a statement released from an unknown location that they would form a "provisional transnational government" to pursue self-rule for the Tamil minority in Sri Lanka. He said a committee was being formed to help the process, headed by an exiled Tamil lawyer in the US, Viswanathan Rudrakumaran.
['New government' for Tamil Tigers, BBC, 16 June 2009
http://news.bbc.co.uk/1/hi/world/south_asia/8102207.stm]

17 June

Following the disbanding of the Presidential Commission of Inquiry into grave human rights abuses, Amnesty International said that the Commission was unable to complete its mandate as no extensions were granted. Of the 16 cases referred, only seven were investigated with reports on five finalized and not a single one resulted in any justice. Amnesty demanded that reports into cases investigated by the Commission be made public immediately.
[Sri Lanka: Presidential Commission of Inquiry fails citizens, Amnesty International, 17 June 2009 -
www.amnesty.org/en/for-media/press-releases/sri-lanka-presidential-commission-inquiry-fails-citizens-20090617]

According to the Sri Lankan government, the Vavuniya-Jaffna A-9 highway was open for private traders to transport essential goods with effect from 17 June 2009.
[A9 opens for private traders, Sri Lanka Government, 17 June 2009
www.priu.gov.lk/news_update/Current_Affairs/ca200906/20090617a9_opens_private_traders.htm]

19 June

Chairman of the Presidential Task Force on Resettlement, Development and Security in the Northern Province, Basil Rajapaksa announced during a meeting with the fishing community at the Karainagar naval camp in Jaffna that the government had decided to lift the ban on fishing in the north. The prohibition on outboard motors of boats had been lifted. Restrictions on fishing have been in force for the past 30 years.
[Government removes fishing restrictions in North, Sri Lanka Government, 22 June 2009
www.priu.gov.lk/news_update/Current_Affairs/ca200906/20090622government_removes_fishing_restrictions.htm]

20 June

An estimated 20,000 people marched in London in support of the Tamil population in Sri Lanka. The demonstration followed a 73-day protest for peace in the country that ended on 17 June 2009 and featured mass sit-ins blocking central London roads.
[Thousands march for Tamil rights, BBC, 20 June 2009 - http://news.bbc.co.uk/1/hi/uk/8110837.stm]

23 June

The European Commission allocated €5 million to provide life-saving humanitarian assistance to IDPs, mostly Tamils in camps in Sri Lanka, through projects to be implemented by NGOs and specialised UN agencies.

June 2009

[*Sri Lanka: European Commission provides €5 million for life-saving emergency humanitarian assistance*, European Commission External Relations, 23 June 2009
http://europa.eu/rapid/pressReleasesAction.do?reference=IP/09/983&format=HTML&aged=0&language=EN&guiLanguage=en]

24 June

A Sri Lankan delegation comprising Presidential Advisor Basil Rajapaksa, Defence Secretary Gotabaya Rajapaksa, and President's Secretary Lalith Weeratunga, assured Indian Foreign Minister S. M. Krishna that the IDPs in the Northern Province will be resettled within 180 days. The delegation also detailed the steps being taken to improve the conditions and facilities for the IDPs in relief centres, such as the provision of schools and text books, introduction of solar-powered telephone booths for easier communication, improved accommodation facilities and health and sanitary services.
[*Govt. committed to resettle IDPs in six months: Sri Lankan delegation assures India*, Sri Lanka Government, 25 June 2009 -
www.priu.gov.lk/news_update/Current_Affairs/ca200906/20090625govt_committed_to_resettle_idp_in_6months.htm]

July 2009

8 July

Five Sri Lankan government doctors who were arrested in May 2009 for giving casualty figures to journalists in the last months of the civil war recanted, claiming they had been under LTTE pressure to exaggerate the civilian death toll. The doctors were presented to the press at the Defence Ministry's media centre while still in custody. Asia-Pacific Director of Amnesty International, Sam Zarifi said the doctors' appearance had been expected and predicted. "Given the track record of the Sri Lankan government, there are very significant grounds to question whether these statements were voluntary and they raise serious concerns whether the doctors were subjected to ill-treatment during weeks of detention", he said.

[*Sri Lankan doctors paraded to recant over 'false' casualty figures*, The Guardian (UK), 8 July 2009 - www.guardian.co.uk/world/2009/jul/08/sri-lanka-doctors-casualty-figures]

9 July

The ICRC announced that it was closing four of its offices in the Eastern Province after the Sri Lankan government told international relief agencies to cut back their activities in the country on the basis that there was no more fighting in the country, despite an estimated 300,000 displaced Tamils still needing food, medicine and help to return home.

[*Sri Lanka orders cuts in aid work*, BBC, 9 July 2009 http://news.bbc.co.uk/1/hi/world/south_asia/8142550.stm]

10 July

Following the Sri Lankan government order to the ICRC to scale back operations, UK's Foreign and Commonwealth Minister Lord Malloch-Brown, said that the end of the conventional conflict in Sri Lanka does not mean that the presence of the ICRC ceases to be necessary, as significant challenges still remain, particularly in relation to the civilians in camps for the IDPs. He urged the Sri Lanka government to continue its dialogue with the ICRC on issues of humanitarian concern, both protection and assistance, and to provide every opportunity for the ICRC to implement its mandate as Sri Lanka takes its first steps towards recovery.

[*Sri Lanka ask Red Cross to scale back operations*, Foreign and Commonwealth Office, 10 July 2009 www.fco.gov.uk/en/newsroom/latest-news/?view=PressS&id=20551605]

15 July

The UN Office of the Humanitarian Coordinator in Sri Lanka reported that during the 27 October 2008 to 10 July 2009 period, 282,380 persons crossed to the Sri Lankan government controlled areas from the Vanni conflict zone. As of 15 July 2009, there were 278,051 displaced people in camps – 260,039 in Vavuniya, 225 in Mannar, 10,956 in Jaffna and 6,831 in Trincomalee. As of 21 June 2009, there were 4,329 IDPs (injured and care givers) in hospitals in various districts. As of 18 June 2009, 5,483 people (Vavuniya Camps: 5,303; Mannar Camps: 17; Jaffna Camps: 163) were released from temporary camps into host families and elders' homes.

[*Joint Humanitarian Update, North-East Sri Lanka*, Report # 01, 3 – 10 July 2009, United Nations Office of the Resident Coordinator and Humanitarian Coordinator, Sri Lanka - www.reliefweb.int/rw/RWFiles2009.nsf/FilesByRWDocUnidFilename/PSLG-7TYD9V-full_report.pdf/$File/full_report.pdf]

July 2009

16 July

International medical agency Medecins Sans Frontieres (MSF) which is working in the Vavuniya and Pampaimadu hospitals, as well as in an MSF hospital located near Menic Farm IDP camps, said medical teams in Vavuniya District have performed more than 5,000 surgeries over five months, most to treat conflict-related injuries. According to MSF head of mission for Sri Lanka Hugues Robert, the population in Vavuniya District nearly doubled with more than 260,000 displaced persons arriving from Vanni and increasing numbers of displaced persons were coming to the hospitals. Many pregnant women and children had developed complications from respiratory illnesses, malnutrition and diarrhoea.

[*Sri Lanka: Hospitals overflowing with patients*, Medecins Sans Frontieres, 16 July 2009 - www.msf.org.uk/sri_lanka_hospitals_overflowing_20090716.news]

28 July

Human Rights Watch called on the Sri Lankan government to immediately release the more than 280,000 internally displaced Tamil civilians held in detention camps in northern Sri Lanka since March 2008 in violation of international law. Only a small number of camp residents, mainly the elderly, have been released to host families and institutions for the elderly. In response to domestic and international criticism, President Mahinda Rajapaksa has tried to justify the detention policy by claiming that anyone in the camps could be a security threat. Human Rights Watch said that the government has not provided any concrete resettlement plans and displaced persons have not received any information about when they might be allowed to return home.

[*Sri Lanka: Free civilians from detention camps*, Human Rights Watch, 28 July 2009 www.hrw.org/en/news/2009/07/28/sri-lanka-free-civilians-detention-camps]

August 2009

7 August

Sri Lanka defence spokesman Keheliya Rambukwella announced that the new leader of the LTTE, Selvarasa Pathmanathan had been arrested "in the Asian region" within the past couple of days and taken to Sri Lanka. Initial reports from Sri Lankan military officials suggested the arrest took place in Thailand, but Thai government spokesman Panitan Wattanayagorn denied Mr Pathmanathan was arrested in his country but conceded there were "reports that he has been travelling in and out of Thailand".

[*New Tamil Tiger head is arrested*, BBC, 7 August 2009   http://news.bbc.co.uk/1/hi/8188900.stm]

19 August

The report of the Committees on Arms Export Controls of UK's House of Commons, revealed that weapons had been licensed by Britain for export to Sri Lanka every year from 1997 onwards, including components, communications equipment, armoured vehicles, naval guns and naval equipment. During the fragile ceasefire beginning in 2002, a wide variety of military equipment and weapons were exported to Sri Lanka. In 2006, when the truce broke down and hostilities began to escalate, Britain was still exporting weapons including air guns, aircraft, military communications equipment, armoured all-wheel drive vehicles, components for machine guns, components for military air engines, components for semi-automatic pistols, small arms ammunition and components for combat aircraft. In the period 1 April 2008 to 31 March 2009, 34 licences were issued for export to Sri Lanka. According to the report, due to the extremely limited access of international observers to Sri Lanka, it is impossible to be certain how many of those weapons were used subsequently against the civilian population when hostilities began to escalate again in 2006.

The Committees made the following recommendations: "We conclude that the policy of assessing licences to Sri Lanka on a case-by-case basis is, in our opinion, appropriate. However, we recommend that the Government should review all existing licences relating to Sri Lanka and provide in its Response an assessment of what implications the situation in Sri Lanka will have on how the Foreign and Commonwealth Office judges the possible future use of strategic exports by that country and the risk that the export licensing criteria might be breached. We further recommend that the Government provide in its Response an assessment of what UK supplied weapons, ammunition, parts and components were used by the Sri Lankan armed forces in the recent military actions against the Tamil Tigers."

Chairman of the committees Roger Berry said Britain must assess more carefully the risk that UK arms exports might be used by those countries in the future in a way that breaches our licensing criteria. "Britain is legally bound by the European Union code of conduct on arms transfers, which restricts the arms trade to countries facing internal conflicts or with poor human rights records and a history of violating international law. The code focuses not on the lethal potential of the weapon but on its end use." Liberal Democrat MP Malcolm Bruce said "With hindsight, Britain's sales did violate the EU code of conduct".

[*Scrutiny of arms export controls (2009)*, Business and Enterprise, Defence, Foreign Affairs and International Development Committees, First Joint Report of Session 2008–09, House of Commons UK, 19 August 2009 - www.publications.parliament.uk/pa/cm200809/cmselect/cmquad/178/178.pdf; *Arms review urged over fears British weapons were used against Tamils*, The Times (UK), 19 August 2009 - www.timesonline.co.uk/tol/news/politics/article6801207.ece]

August 2009

25 August

UK's Channel 4 televised pictures showing Sri Lankan troops summarily executing persons who were naked and blindfolded with hands tied behind their backs. Journalists for Democracy in Sri Lanka, which obtained the film said the victims were Tamils and the executions were filmed in January 2009 during the period of the war, when international and independent local media were prevented by the Sri Lankan government from covering the conflict zone.

[*Execution video: is this evidence of 'war crimes' in Sri Lanka?*, Channel 4 TV (UK), 25 August 2009 - www.channel4.com/news/; *Video evidence of extra-judicial executions in Sri Lanka*, Statement of Journalists for Democracy in Sri Lanka, 25 August 2009 - www.tamilnet.com/img/publish/2009/08/JDS_letter.pdf]

September 2009

7 September

James Elder, the official spokesman for UNICEF in Sri Lanka was ordered to leave the country. The Controller of Immigration and Emigration P. B. Abeykoon said that the government revoked Mr Elder's visa because of adverse remarks made to the media. In May 2009 Mr Elder had spoken of the "unimaginable hell" suffered by children caught in the final stages of the war and the "horrendous and disproportionate" suffering of children when civilians caught on the front line emerged after the conflict. He had also called on the government to lift tight restrictions on access for humanitarian groups to about 280,000 mostly Tamil refugees forcibly held in internment camps.

[*UNICEF worker James Elder expelled from Sri Lanka over media comments*, The Times (UK), 7 September 2009 – www.timesonline.co.uk/tol/news/world/asia/article6824039.ece]

8 September

UN Secretary-General Ban Ki-moon strongly regretted Sri Lankan government's decision to expel UNICEF Spokesman James Elder and expressed full confidence in the work of the UN in Sri Lanka, which includes making public statements when necessary in an effort to save lives and prevent grave humanitarian problems. He said that the UN is working impartially to assist the people of Sri Lanka, and the government should be supporting and cooperating with its efforts.

[Statement of the Spokesperson for the Secretary-General on Sri Lanka, 8 September 2009 - www.un.org/apps/sg/sgstats.asp?nid=4053]

11 September

UK newspaper *The Guardian* revealed that senior UN diplomat Peter Mackay, an Australian citizen, was expelled from Sri Lanka in July 2009 for providing detailed rebuttals of the Sri Lankan government's "wartime propaganda" during the final battles against the LTTE. Mr. Mackay who worked as a field operative for the UN Office for Project Services (UNOPS), the technical arm of the UN, was given two weeks to leave the country, despite having a visa until the summer of 2010. He was monitoring the conflict, had put together briefings for embassies in Colombo that challenged Sri Lanka's official civilian death toll and its arrangements for relief operations. He played a key role in keeping the outside world informed about the number of civilians killed in the final months of the war – deaths that Sri Lanka was keen to play down. Mr. Mackay collected high-resolution satellite images showing that the number of people trapped on beaches where the LTTE made their last stand was far higher than that claimed by the government. The data showed that not only were more people in danger than the government admitted, but that the food and medicine sent to the 'civilian safe zone' were inadequate.

[*Sri Lankan government evicted UN diplomat during Tamil Tiger endgame*, The Guardian (UK), 11 September 2009 - www.guardian.co.uk/world/2009/sep/11/sri-lanka-tamil-tigers-un]

English Catholic Bishops John Rawsthorne of Sheffield and John Arnold of Westminster, who returned from a visit to refugee camps in Sri Lanka, called for the end of forced confinement of nearly 300,000 Tamil survivors of the country's conflict. They said there is serious overcrowding and inadequate food and health services in the camps.

[*Sri Lanka: Bishops say all must be allowed home*, CAFOD, 11 September 2009 - www.cafod.org.uk/news/sri-lanka-2009-09-11]

September 2009

14 September

In its Travel Advice on Sri Lanka, UK's Foreign and Commonwealth Office (FCO) advised against all travel to the north of Sri Lanka,and all but essential travel to most parts of eastern Sri Lanka, including the districts of Batticaloa (all areas), Trincomalee (rural areas), and Amparai (north and eastern areas). The FCO said all territory in Sri Lanka is now under government control, however, politically motivated violence, abductions and criminality persisted throughout the country, particularly in the north and east. It also said that the government maintains its State of Emergency, under which it has extensive anti-terrorism powers and increased security measures including checkpoints remain throughout the country.

[*Travel Advice: Sri Lanka*, Foreign and Commonwealth Office (UK), 14 September 2009 - www.fco.gov.uk/en/travelling-and-living-overseas/travel-advice-by-country/asia-oceania/sri-lanka/?ta=travelSummary&pg=1]

15 September

In her opening address to the 12th Session of the UN Human Rights Council, the High Commissioner for Human Rights Navi Pillay noted that an "intolerable" number of displaced people continue to live in camps, adding that in the case of Sri Lanka "internally displaced persons are effectively detained under conditions of internment."

[*Tackling impunity and discrimination among top priorities for UN rights chief*, UN News Centre, 15 September 2009 - www.un.org/apps/news/story.asp?NewsID=32049&Cr=pillay&Cr1=]

At the 12th Session of the UN Human Rights Council, UN Special Representative for Children and Armed Conflict, Radhika Coomaraswamy expressed concern about the fate of internally displaced children who still remain in camps in the north of Sri Lanka, many of them kept against their will. She said many children are separated from their families and do not have complete access to humanitarian assistance.

[*Statement by UN Special Representative of the Secretary General Radhika Coomaraswamy*, 12th Session of the Human Rights Council, 15 September 2009 - www.un.org/children/conflict/english/statements.html]

17 September

UN Special Rapporteur on extrajudicial, summary or arbitrary executions Philip Alston said in a statement that the four separate investigations undertaken by the Sri Lankan government into the authenticity of a video of alleged extrajudicial executions by Sri Lankan soldiers shown by the British Channel 4 TV in August 2009 were not "thorough" or "impartial", and noted that two of the experts were members of the Sri Lanka army. Mr. Alston called for an independent and impartial investigation.

[*Sri Lanka should permit impartial probe into alleged execution video*, UN News Centre, 17 September 2009 www.un.org/apps/news/story.asp?NewsID=32085&Cr=sri+lanka&Cr1=]

18 September

After touring northern Sri Lanka, UN Under-Secretary-General for Political Affairs B. Lynn Pascoe said that more than 280,000 IDPs living in government-run camps lacked basic rights of freedom of movement, and the country is not making the expected progress towards a lasting peace in the wake of the end to fighting. He declared that this kind of closed regime goes directly against the principles

September 2009

under which UN works in assisting IDPs around the world and urged the government to allow those IDPs who have completed the screening process to leave the camps as they choose, and for those people remaining to be able to exit the camps during the day and to freely meet with family and friends in other sites.

[*UN political chief voices concern about displaced after wrapping up visit to Sri Lanka*, UN News Centre, 18 September 2009 - www.un.org/apps/news/story.asp?NewsID=32112&Cr=sri+lanka&Cr1=]

22 September

SLFP (M) Leader Mangala Samaraweera alleged in the Sri Lankan Parliament that 30 to 40 persons were abducted daily from IDP camps in northern Sri Lanka and disappeared. He said the welfare camps were virtual prisons and demanded that an opposition delegation should be allowed to visit the camps to assess the situation. Chief Government Whip Dinesh Gunawardane denied the allegation of abduction and disappearance.

[*IDPs are abducted or disappear: Mangala*, Daily Mirror (Sri Lanka), 23 September 2009 www.dailymirror.lk/DM_BLOG/Sections/frmNewsDetailView.aspx?ARTID=62350]

29 September

UN Secretary-General Ban Ki-Moon said he remained very concerned about the very slow pace of releases of Tamil refugees held in camps and warned during talks with the Sri Lankan Prime Minister Ratnasiri Wickramanayake in New York that Sri Lanka risks creating bitterness if it fails to rapidly resettle them. The Secretary-General's Representative on the human rights of IDPs Walter Kälin noted that international law allows for internment during the height of conflict if legitimate and imperative security concerns exist, but it must not last longer than absolutely necessary to respond to those security concerns. Internment decisions must further be made on an individual rather than a group basis, he said.

[*UN rights envoy voices concern for 250,000 displaced Sri Lankans trapped in camps*, UN News Centre, 29 September 2009 - www.un.org/apps/news/story.asp?NewsID=32341&Cr=sri+lanka&Cr1=]

October 2009

22 October

In a report to Congress, the US State Department detailed extensive abuses and violations of the laws of war committed by both Sri Lanka government forces and the LTTE from January to May 2009. The report addressed the following categories of incidents:

1) <u>Children in armed conflict</u> - On numerous occasions during January to May 2009, the LTTE took both male and female children, some as young as 12, to join LTTE cadres.

2) <u>Harm to civilians and civilian objects</u> - Sources alleged that a significant number of deaths and injuries incurred at the time of attack were likely never recorded. Senior Sri Lankan officials denied that the Sri Lanka government forces shelled the 'civilian safe zone' or targeted hospitals and were not responsible for any civilian casualties. However, sources alleged that the majority of shelling in the 'civilian safe zone' was from Sri Lanka government forces. The government announced that it would observe a 48-hour ceasefire on two occasions to allow civilians to move into areas in which they would not be subject to shelling. Incident reports suggest, however, that the government may have begun shelling before the end of the second 48-hour ceasefire. Reports also indicated that the LTTE forcibly prevented the escape of IDPs and used them as "human shields".

3) <u>Killing of captives or combatants seeking to surrender</u> - A number of sources alleged that the Sri Lanka government committed unlawful killings. Multiple reports alleged that in the final few days of fighting, senior LTTE leaders contacted international representatives in an effort to broker a surrender but were killed after they allegedly reached a surrender agreement with the Sri Lanka government.

4) <u>Disappearances</u> - According to reports, Sri Lanka government forces or Sri Lanka government-supported paramilitaries abducted and in some instances then killed Tamil civilians, particularly children and young men. Sources reported that these individuals were taken to undisclosed locations without any further information being provided to relatives. IDP checkpoints and camps were alleged to be particularly vulnerable areas, with a heavy military presence hindering the ability of international organizations to conduct protection monitoring and confidential IDP interviews.

5) <u>Humanitarian conditions</u>   Reports include instances of severe food shortages; malnutrition, particularly among the very young and old; as well as surgeries being performed with little or no anaesthetic. The Sri Lanka government pledged to provide sufficient food and medical supplies to people in IDP camps and to those trapped in the 'civilian safe zone'. However, most reports point to significant gaps between food, medicine, and clean water needs and the available supplies in the 'civilian safe zone' and IDP camps.

[*Report to Congress on incidents during the recent conflict in Sri Lanka*, US State Department, 22 October 2009 www.state.gov/documents/organization/131025.pdf]

November 2009

3 November

UN Special Rapporteur on extrajudicial, summary or arbitrary executions Professor Philip Alston commissioned Jeff Spivack an expert in forensic video analysis, Peter Diaczuc, an expert in firearms evidence and Dr Daniel Spitz, a forensic pathologist, to conduct an analysis of the digital video/audio recording purportedly depicting executions of Tamils by Sri Lanka armed forces personnel, broadcast by UK Channel 4 TV on 25 August 2009. The video appeared to depict Sri Lanka military members shooting two unidentified bound and blindfolded individuals in the head at close range with an AK-47 variant or similar assault rifle, as well as the presence of several other unidentified deceased or dying individuals.

[Technical Note prepared by the Special Rapporteur and Appendix to the Technical Note containing the opinions of the three experts, UN Special Rapporteur on extrajudicial, summary or arbitrary executions www2.ohchr.org/english/issues/executions/index.htm]

23 November

President Mahinda Rajapaksa declared his intention of appealing to the people of Sri Lanka for a mandate to hold office for a further term, by election under Paragraph 3A of Article 31 of the Constitution.

[Proclamation by President Mahinda Rajapaksa, Government Gazette Extraordinary, No. 1629/08, 23 November 2009 -
www.priu.gov.lk/news_update/Current_Affairs/ca200911/gazette20091123_english.pdf]

27 November

Commissioner of Elections Dayananda Dissanayake announced that the Presidential Election will be held on 26 January 2010. He said nominations for the election will be accepted on 17 December 2009 between 9 am and 11 am.

[*Presidential Election on January 26, 2010*, News Line, Sri Lanka government, 27 November 2009 -
www.priu.gov.lk/news_update/Current_Affairs/ca200911/20091127presidential_election.htm]

29 November

Former Sri Lankan army commander Sarath Fonseka announced his candidature for the Presidential election challenging incumbent Mahinda Rajapaksa. Gen. Fonseka, who quit as the Chief of Defence Staff three weeks ago following a conflict with President Rajapaksa, said he would be the joint candidate of the opposition parties, including the UNP and the JVP.

[*Fonseka announces candidature against Rajapaksa*, Outlook (India), 29 November 2009
http://news.outlookindia.com/item.aspx?670215]

December 2009

1 December

After the Sri Lanka government announced that it would allow freedom of movement for the Tamil IDP who were held in internment camps in the Vanni, at least 9,300 people moved out of the camps to visit their relatives after registering themselves with the relevant authorities.

[*Govt allows Freedom of Movement for IDPs*, News Line, Sri Lanka government, 2 December 2009 - www.priu.gov.lk/news_update/Current_Affairs/ca200912/20091202govt_allows_freedom_of_moveme nt.htm]

Yolanda Foster, Amnesty International's expert on Sri Lanka, called on the Sri Lankan government to make good on its declared intentions and free some 120,000 Tamil IDPs in camps in the Vanni unconditionally and permanently, accompanied by assurance that they are not subjected to further questioning or re-arrest in new locations. The statement was issued after media reports suggested that some people may be asked to return to the camps after only 15 days. Amnesty also expressed concern over the lack of assistance for those released from the camps and urged the government to provide the IDPs with clear information about their rights, their legal status and procedures for tracing family members.

[*Sri Lankan government must permanently release all civilians*, Amnesty International, 1 December 2009 www.amnesty.org/en/news-and-updates/news/sri-lankan-government-must-permanently-release-all-civilians-20091202]

4 December

Sri Lanka's Minister of Resettlement and Disaster Relief Services, Abdul Risath Bathiyutheen said that the 100,000 Muslims expelled from the Northern Province by the LTTE in October 1990 and living in Puttalam will be resettled in their home areas.

[*Resettling of expelled Northern Muslims to begin on Dec. 26*, Peace Secretariat for Muslims, 4 December 2009 www.peacemuslims.org/print.php?pageid=20&id=1361&vType=]

13 December

In an interview to Sri Lankan newspaper *The Sunday Leader*, former army commander Sarath Fonseka accused Defence Secretary Gotabaya Rajapakse of giving the order to kill the LTTE leaders who surrendered on 18 May 2009. Political head of the LTTE Balasingham Mahendran (Nadesan), head of the LTTE peace secretariat Seevaratnam Prabhakaran (Pulidevan) and senior commander of the military wing Thambirajah Ramesh were killed by Sri Lankan troops while attempting surrender following negotiations with senior government officers and carrying a white flag as instructed. General Fonseka said that Gotabaya Rajapaksa gave orders to Shavendra Silva, Commander of the Army's 58th Division, not to accommodate any LTTE leaders attempting surrender and that "they must all be killed."

[*"Gota ordered them to be shot" – General Sarath Fonseka*, The Sunday Leader (Sri Lanka), 13 December 2009 www.thesundayleader.lk/2009/12/13/%e2%80%9cgota-ordered-them-to-be-shot%e2%80%9d-%e2%80%93-general-sarath-fonseka/#comment-6776]

17 December

Twenty three candidates - 18 from recognized political parties and five from independent groups - handed over nominations for the presidential election to the Elections Commissioner. The Commissioner rejected the nomination of Peter Nelson Perera of the Sri Lanka Progressive Front over discrepancies in the nomination papers.

December 2009

[Development challenge easy for me   President, Daily News (Sri Lanka), 18 December 2009 -
www.dailynews.lk/2009/12/18/news01.asp]

26 December

Transparency International Sri Lanka (TISL) warned that if lessons are not drawn over the failure of the Sri Lanka government in the tsunami reconstruction process and immediate action taken, the post-conflict development in the north and the east will be jeopardized. According to TISL, a sum of US $471,931,440 has gone missing from the tsunami funds (March 2007 data: funds promised by donors - $2,126,771,858; funds actually provided – $1,075,375,348; funds spent on projects $603,443,908). Sri Lankan government officials are unable to explain the missing amount and according to the Auditor General's Department, no audit has been conducted on funds received for tsunami reconstruction process since 2005. TISL called for an audit to explain the utilization of the money received; steps to remedy the existing problems in the tsunami recovery process with the participation of the public; and appointment of an independent commission to review any remaining issues relating to the recovery process.

[Lessons to be learnt from tsunami reconstruction process for the development of the north and the east of Sri Lanka, Transparency International Sri Lanka, 26 December 2009 - www.tisrilanka.org/?p=2994]

2010

1 January

The UN Office of the Humanitarian Coordinator in Sri Lanka reported that 108,106 people were in IDP camps (Vavuniya 102,403; Mannar 2,096; Jaffna 3,607) as of 31 December 2009. Between 5 August 2009 and 31 December 2009, 155,966 persons were returned to Jaffna, Vavuniya, Mannar, Trincomalee, Batticaloa, Mullaitivu, Kilinochchi, Amparai, Kandy and Polonnaruwa districts. As of 31 December 2009, 28,854 people were released from IDP camps into host families and elders' homes, majority of who were elders, people with disabilities and other vulnerable groups.
[*Joint Humanitarian Update, North-East Sri Lanka*, Report # 16, 19 December 2009 – 1 January 2010, United Nations Office of the Resident Coordinator and Humanitarian Coordinator, Sri Lanka www.reliefweb.int/rw/RWFiles2010.nsf/FilesByRWDocUnidFilename/LSGZ-7ZMJMW-full_report.pdf/$File/full_report.pdf]

7 January

UN Special Rapporteur on extrajudicial, summary or arbitrary executions, Philip Alston announced that reports by three independent experts strongly point to the authenticity of a videotape released by Channel 4 in Britain which appears to show the summary execution of bound, blindfolded, and naked Tamils by Sri Lankan soldiers.

Peter Diaczuk, the expert in firearms evidence, concluded that the recoil, movement of the weapon and the shooter, and the gases expelled from the muzzle in both apparent shootings were consistent with firing live ammunition, and not with shooting blank cartridges. Dr. Daniel Spitz, the forensic pathologist, found that the footage appeared authentic, especially with respect to the two individuals who are shown being shot in the head at close range. He found that the body reaction, movement, and blood evidence was entirely consistent with what would be expected in such shootings. Jeff Spivack, the expert in forensic video analysis, found no evidence of breaks in continuity in the video, no additional video layers, and no evidence of image manipulation.

Mr. Alston added that the independent experts' analyses also systematically rebutted most of the arguments relied upon by Sri Lanka's experts in support of their contention that the video was faked. Given these conclusions, and in light of the persistent flow of other allegations of extrajudicial executions by both sides during the closing phases of the war, Mr. Alston called for the establishment of an independent inquiry for an impartial investigation into war crimes and other grave violations of international humanitarian and human rights law allegedly committed in Sri Lanka.
[*UN expert concludes that Sri Lankan video is authentic, calls for an independent war crimes investigation*, Office of the UN High Commissioner for Human Rights, 7 January 2010 www.ohchr.org/EN/NewsEvents/Pages/DisplayNews.aspx?NewsID=9706&LangID=E]

15 January

The UN Office of the Humanitarian Coordinator in Sri Lanka reported that 106,123 people were in IDP camps (Vavuniya 100,566; Mannar 1950 Jaffna 3607) as of 15 January 2010. Between 5 August 2009 and 15 January 2010, 158,562 persons were returned to Jaffna, Vavuniya, Mannar, Trincomalee, Batticaloa, Mullaitivu, Kilinochchi, Amparai, Kandy and Polonnaruwa districts. As of 14

January 2010

January 2010, 28,973 people were released from IDP camps into host families and elders' homes, majority of who were elders, people with disabilities and other vulnerable groups.
[*Joint Humanitarian Update, North-East Sri Lanka*, Report # 17, 2-15 January 2010, United Nations Office of the Resident Coordinator and Humanitarian Coordinator, Sri Lanka - www.reliefweb.int/rw/RWFiles2010.nsf/FilesByRWDocUnidFilename/VVOS-82ASUC-full_report.pdf/$File/full_report.pdf]

16 January
In its preliminary findings following hearings in Dublin from 14 to 16 January 2010, the Permanent People's Tribunal on Sri Lanka concluded that the Sri Lankan government was guilty of war crimes and crimes against humanity. The Rome-based Permanent Peoples' Tribunal (PPT) which constituted the Sri Lanka tribunal is an international opinion tribunal, independent from any State authority. It examines cases regarding violations of human rights and the rights of peoples. The Permanent People's Tribunal on Sri Lanka composed of the following panel members: François Houtart (Chairperson), Prof. Emeritus of the Catholic University of Louvain (Belgium); Daniel Feierstein, Director of the Centre for Genocide Studies at the Universidad Nacional de Tres de Febrero, Argentina; Denis Halliday, Former Assistant Secretary-General of the United Nations; Mary Lawlor, Director, Front Line, International Foundation for the Protection of Human Rights Defenders, Dublin; Francesco Martone, Leading activist in the non-governmental sector and an ecologist; Nawalal Saadawi, Former advisor for UN Women's Programme in Africa and Middle East; Rajindar Sachar, Former Chief Justice, High Court of Delhi; Sulak Sivaraksa, Thai Buddhist peace campaigner and writer; Gianni Tognoni, Secretary General, Permanent People's Tribunal, Rome; Øystein Tveter, Scholar of International Law and member of the People's Tribunal on the Philippines.

The Tribunal distinguished three different kinds of human rights violations committed by the Sri Lankan government from 2002 (the beginning of the ceasefire agreement between the government and the LTTE) to the present:

1) Forced "disappearances" of targeted individuals from the Tamil population.
2) Crimes committed in the re-starting of the war (2006-2009), particularly during the last months of the war:
   - Bombing civilian objectives like hospitals, schools and other non-military targets;
   - Bombing government-proclaimed 'civilian safe zones';
   - Withholding of food, water, and health facilities in war zones;
   - Use of heavy weaponry, banned weapons and air-raids;
   - Using food and medicine as a weapon of war;
   - Torture and execution of captured or surrendered LTTE combatants and supporters;
   - Torture;
   - Rape and sexual violence against women;
   - Deportations and forcible transfer of individuals and families;
   - Desecrating the dead.
3) Human rights violations in the IDP camps during and after the end of the war:
   - Shooting of Tamil citizens and LTTE supporters;
   - Forced disappearances;
   - Rape;

January 2010

- Malnutrition;
- Lack of medical supplies.

The Tribunal concluded that the actions included under point 2 above clearly constitute "war crimes" committed by the Sri Lankan government, its security forces and aligned paramilitary forces, as defined under the Geneva Conventions and in the Rome Statute, with regard to sections in Article 8. The Tribunal also concluded that the actions included under the points 1 (forced disappearances) and 3 (violations committed in the IDP camps during and after the war) clearly constitute "crimes against humanity", as defined in the Rome Statute, Article 7. The Tribunal acknowledged the importance of continuing investigation into the possibility of genocide.[2]

The Tribunal stressed the responsibility of the UN Member States that have not complied with their moral obligation to seek justice for the violations of human rights committed during the last period of war. After repeated pleas, and in spite of the appalling conditions experienced by Tamils, the UN Human Rights Council and the UN Security Council failed to establish an independent commission of inquiry to investigate those responsible for the atrocities committed due to political pressure exerted by certain UN members.

The Tribunal highlighted the conduct of the EU in undermining the ceasefire agreement of 2002. In spite of being aware of the detrimental consequences to a peace process in the making, the EU decided – under pressure from the US and the UK - to list the Tamil Resistance Movement, which included the LTTE, as a terrorist organization in 2006. This decision allowed the Sri Lankan government to breach the ceasefire agreement and re-start military operations leading to the massive violations listed above. The Tribunal pointed to the full responsibility of those governments, led by the US, that are conducting the so-called "Global War on Terror" in providing political endorsement of the conduct of the Sri Lankan government and armed forces in a war that is primarily targeted against the Tamil people.

The Tribunal also pointed to the direct responsibility of various countries in providing the Sri Lankan government with weapons. Some of these weapons are banned by conventions such as the Convention on Certain Conventional Weapons (CCW), and others. In addition, some of those countries also trained Sri Lankan military forces during the ceasefire period.

The Tribunal made several recommendations, including the following:
- The appointment of a UN Special Rapporteur for Sri Lanka to investigate and identify responsibilities for human rights violations, violations of humanitarian law and war crimes committed by all parties in conflict;
- The establishment of an independent group of eminent persons to investigate the responsibilities of the international community in the disruption of the ceasefire agreement and subsequent war crimes and crimes against humanity and provision of the Sri Lankan government with weapons during the ceasefire;

---

[2] The Rome Statute of the International Criminal Court includes the definitions of "war crimes", "crimes against humanity" and "genocide". The Statute may be accessed at http://untreaty.un.org/cod/icc/statute/romefra.htm; Geneva Conventions may be accessed at www2.ohchr.org/English/law/.

January 2010

- The establishment of a field office of the UNHRC to allow for independent monitoring of the human rights situation of the Tamil people, and the implementation of Tamil rehabilitation and resettlement programmes, as well as measures aimed at reinstating fundamental rights, freedoms and the rule of law;
- The creation of an inter-governmental and inter-agency task force to coordinate donor agencies' activities to support peace and reconciliation processes, landmine clearance, rehabilitation and post-war reconstruction, subject to the rights and wishes of the Tamils.

[People's Tribunal on Sri Lanka, Conducted by Permanent People's Tribunal (Rome), Trinity College, Dublin, Ireland, 14-16 January 2010 - www.ifpsl.org/images/files/peoples_tribunal_on_srilanka.pdf]

18 January

The Colombo Magistrates Court ordered the police to release the five Tamil doctors who served in Kilinochchi and Mullaitivu districts during the last stages of war, if no evidence is found against them. Doctors Thangamuthu Sathiyamoorthy, Thurairajah Vartharajah, Ilanchelian Vallavan, V. Shanmugarajah and N. Ketheesh were accused by the Sri Lanka government of providing false information on casualty figures to international media. They were released on bail in August 2009 and later allowed to work in government hospitals. The police informed the court that investigations whether they committed any offence under Emergency Regulations were continuing.
[*Court orders release of Vanni doctors*, BBC, 18 January 2010 -
www.bbc.co.uk/sinhala/news/story/2010/01/100118_vanni_doctors.shtml]

26 January

Mahinda Rajapaksa was re-elected as the Sixth Executive President of Sri Lanka. He received 6,015,934 votes (57.88%) while Sarath Fonseka polled 4,173,185 votes (40.15%). Twenty two persons contested the election. The turn-out was 74.49% for the whole island, while the turn-out was only 25.66% in Jaffna electoral district and 40.33% in the Vanni electoral district (See Annex 1 for election results).
[*It's Mahinda*, Daily News (Sri Lanka), 27 January 2010 - www.dailynews.lk/2010/01/28/pol01.asp]

27 January

The outcome of the presidential election was rejected by General Sarath Fonseka. He said that he would institute legal action challenging the outcome of the ballot. In a letter to the Elections Commissioner, he accused President Mahinda Rajapaksa of using the state media to attack him, misappropriating public funds for the election campaign and preventing displaced Tamils from voting.
[*Fonseka rejects Sri Lanka election win for Rajapaksa*, BBC, 27 January 2010 -
http://news.bbc.co.uk/1/hi/8482963.stm; *Fonseka rejects Lanka poll result, says he fears arrest*, Yahoo News, 28 January 2009 - http://in.news.yahoo.com/48/20100128/1248/twl-fonseka-rejects-lanka-poll-result-sa.html]

29 January

The US-based Committee to Protect Journalists (CPJ) expressed alarmed by reports that journalists in Sri Lanka have been subjected to government intimidation, arrests, censorship, and harassment in the aftermath of the presidential election. CPJ's Asia Programme Coordinator Bob Dietz that reports had been received of government retribution against journalists who sided with the opposition in

January 2010

the election. CPJ called on President Mahinda Rajapaksa to ensure the safety of all journalists in Sri Lanka, and to use his new mandate to reverse the repressive trends of the past several years
[*Journalists in Sri Lanka face intimidation, censorship*, Committee to Protect Journalists (US), 29 January 2010 http://cpj.org/2010/01/journalists-in-sri-lanka-face-intimidation-censors.php]

Annex 1

Sri Lanka

Presidential Election Results 2010[1]

26 January 2010 – Electoral Districts

Province	Electoral District	Mahinda Rajapaksa		Sarath Fonseka		Votes		
		Total Votes	%	Total Votes	%	Total Registered	Total Polled	% Polled
Central	Kandy	406,636	54.16	329,492	43.89	970,456	759,486	78.26
	Matale	157,953	59.74	100,513	38.01	342,684	267,085	77.94
	Nuwara Eliya	180,604	52.14	151,604	43.77	457,137	352,844	77.19
Eastern	Batticaloa	146,057	68.93	55,663	26.27	333,644	216,287	64.83
	Amparai	153,105	49.94	146,912	47.92	420,835	309,474	73.54
	Trincomalee	87,661	54.09	69,752	43.04	241,133	164,504	68.22
Northern	Jaffna[2]	113,877	63.84	44,154	24.75	721,359	185,132	25.66
	Vanni[3]	70,367	66.86	28,740	27.31	266,975	107,680	40.33
Southern	Galle	386,971	63.69	211,633	34.83	761,815	611,386	80.25
	Matara	296,155	65.53	148,510	32.86	578,858	454,954	78.60
	Hambantota	226,887	67.21	105,336	31.20	421,186	339,782	80.67
Western	Colombo	614,740	52.93	533,022	45.90	1,521,854	1,172,776	77.06
	Gampaha	718,716	61.66	434,506	37.28	1,474,464	1,174,608	79.66
	Kalutara	412,562	63.08	327,594	35.46	813,233	658,790	81.01
North Western	Kurunegala	582,784	63.08	327,594	35.46	1,183,649	930,537	78.62
	Puttalam	201,981	58.70	136,233	39.59	495,575	346,999	70.02
North Central	Anuradhapura	298,448	66.32	143,761	31.94	579,261	453,823	78.35
	Polonnaruwa	144,889	64.92	75,026	33.62	280,337	224,647	80.13
Uva	Badulla	237,579	52.23	198,835	44.55	574,814	452,377	78.70
	Moneragala	158,435	69.01	66,803	29.10	300,642	231,856	77.12
Sabragamuva	Ratnapura	377,734	63.76	203,566	34.36	734,651	596,856	81.24
	Kegalle	296,639	61.80	174,877	36.44	613,938	483,568	78.76
Total		6,015,934	57.88	4,173,185	40.15	14,088,500	10,495,451	74.49

Source: Department of Elections, Sri Lanka - www.slelections.gov.lk/

1 – Twenty two persons contested the presidential election, but only the results of the two main contestants are included in this table. All the other contestants together received only 2.92% of the votes.

2 – The Jaffna electoral district includes the administrative districts of Jaffna and Kilinochchi.

3 – The Vanni electoral district includes the administrative districts of Mullaitivu, Mannar and Vavuniya.

Annex 2

Sri Lanka
General Election Results 2010
8 April 2010 – Electoral Districts

Electoral District	UPFA		UNP		DNA		TNA		Total		
	Votes polled	Seats	Votes polled	Seats	Votes polled	Seats	Votes polled	Seats	Votes polled[3]	%	Seats
Colombo	480,896	10	339,750	7	110,683	2			989,729	65.03	19
Gampaha	589,476	12	266,523	5	69,747	1			980,467	66.50	18
Kalutara	313,836	7	139,596	2	36,722	1			544,606	66.97	10
Kandy	339,819	8	192,798	4	23,728	0			617,559	63.64	12
Matale	131,069	4	55,737	1	7,636	0			215,060	62.76	5
Nuwara Eliya	149,111	5	96,885	2	3,984	0			303,470	66.38	7
Galle	305,307	7	120,101	2	33,663	1			485,401	63.72	10
Matara	213,937	6	91,114	2	20,465	0			341,871	59.06	8
Hambantota	174,808	5	83,027	2	19,186	0			289,294	68.69	7
Jaffna[1]	47,622	3	12,624	1	201	0	65,119	5	168,277	23.33	9
Vanni[2]	37,522	2	12,783	1	301	0	41,673	3	117,185	43.89	6
Batticaloa	62,009	1	22,935	1	324	0	66,235	3	195,367	58.56	5
Digamadulla	132,096	4	90,757	2	2,917	0	26,895	1	272,462	64.74	7
Trincomalee	59,784	2	39,691	1	2,519	0	33,268	1	149,982	62.20	4
Kurunegala	429,316	10	213,713	5	26,440	0			725,566	61.30	15
Puttalam	167,769	6	81,152	2	8,792	0			280,354	56.57	8
Anuradhapura	221,204	7	80,360	2	18,129	0			355,468	61.37	9
Polonnaruwa	118,694	4	45,732	1	6,457	0			186,269	66.44	5
Badulla	203,689	6	112,886	2	15,768	0			373,847	65.04	8
Moneragala	120,634	4	28,892	1	9,018	0			169,640	56.43	5
Ratnapura	305,327	7	125,076	3	11,053	0			480,395	65.39	10
Kegalle	242,463	7	104,925	2	13,518	0			388,420	63.27	9
Total		127		51		5		13			196
National List		17		9		2		1			29
Grand Total	4,843,886	144	2,357,057	60	440,950	7	233,190	14	8,630689	61.26	225

Source: Department of Elections, Sri Lanka - www.slelections.gov.lk/

UPFA – United People's Freedom Alliance (Leader: Mahinda Rajapaksa)

UNP – United National Party (Leader: Ranil Wickremasinghe)

DNA – Democratic National Alliance (Leader: Sarath Fonseka)

TNA – Tamil National Alliance (Contested under name of Ilankai Thamil Arasu Katchi (Leader: R. Sampanthan)

Annex 3

Map 1

Sri Lankan government declared Civilian Safe Zone - 21 January 2009

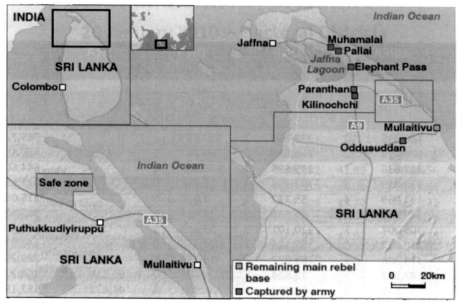

Source: BBC 21 January 2009 - http://news.bbc.co.uk/1/hi/world/south_asia/7842612.stm

Map 2

Sri Lankan government declared Civilian Safe Zone - 21 January 2009

Source: Ministry of Defence, Sri Lanka

Map 3

Civilian Safe Zone declared by the Security Force Headquarters, Vanni – 12 February 2009

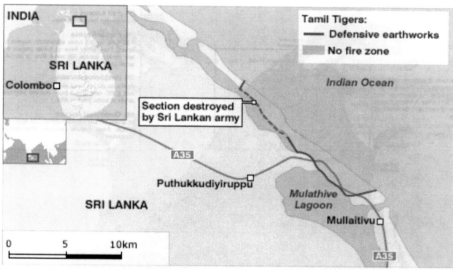

Source: BBC – 1 May 2009 - http://news.bbc.co.uk/1/hi/world/south_asia/8028863.stm

Map 4

Civilian Safe Zone declared by the Security Force Headquarters, Vanni – 12 February 2009

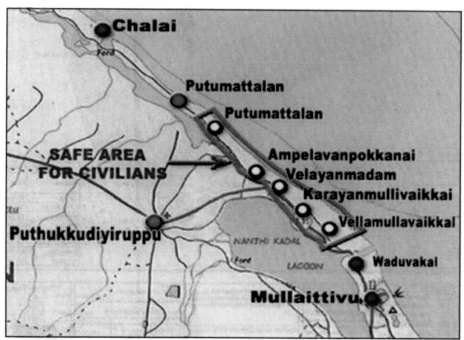

Source: Ministry of Defence, Sri Lanka

Annex 3

Map 5

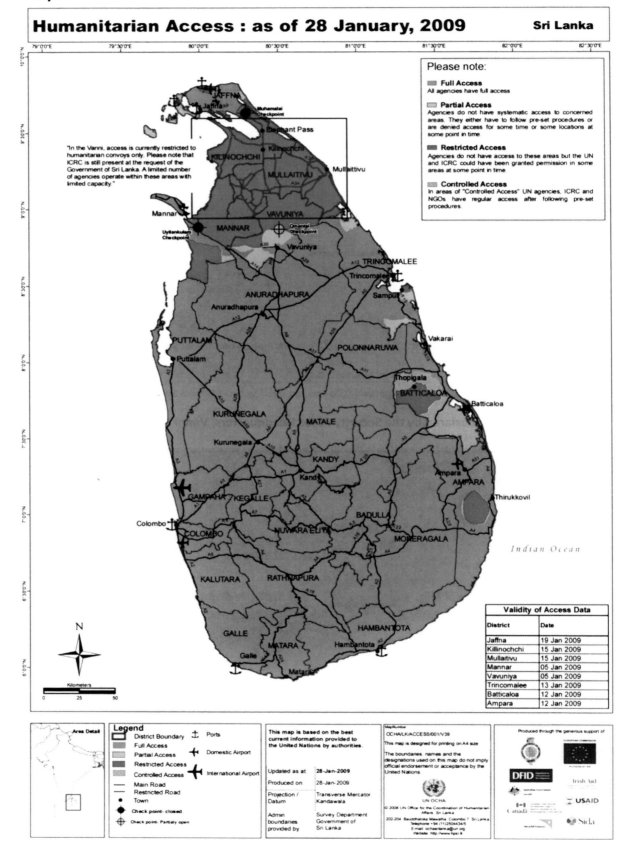

Humanitarian Access : as of 28 January, 2009   Sri Lanka

Please note:

Full Access
All agencies have full access

Partial Access
Agencies do not have systematic access to concerned areas. They either have to follow pre-set procedures or are denied access for some time or some locations at some point in time

Restricted Access
Agencies do not have access to these areas but the UN and ICRC could have been granted permission in some areas at some point in time

Controlled Access
In areas of "Controlled Access" UN agencies, ICRC and NGOs have regular access after following pre-set procedures.

"In the Vanni, access is currently restricted to humanitarian convoys only. Please note that ICRC is still present at the request of the Government of Sri Lanka. A limited number of agencies operate within these areas with limited capacity."

Validity of Access Data

District	Date
Jaffna	19 Jan 2009
Killinochchi	15 Jan 2009
Mullaitivu	15 Jan 2009
Mannar	05 Jan 2009
Vavuniya	05 Jan 2009
Trincomalee	13 Jan 2009
Batticaloa	12 Jan 2009
Ampara	12 Jan 2009

Legend

- District Boundary
- Full Access
- Partial Access
- Restricted Access
- Controlled Access
- Main Road
- Restricted Road
- Town
- Check point- closed
- Check point- Partially open
- Ports
- Domestic Airport
- International Airport

This map is based on the best current information provided to the United Nations by authorities.

Updated as at	28-Jan-2009
Produced on	28-Jan-2009
Projection / Datum	Transverse Mercator Kandawala
Admin boundaries provided by	Survey Department Government of Sri Lanka

MapNumber
OCHA/LK/ACCESS/001/V39

This map is designed for printing on A4 size

The boundaries, names and the designations used on this map do not imply official endorsement or acceptance by the United Nations.

© 2008 UN Office for the Coordination of Humanitarian Affairs, Sri Lanka
202-204 Bauddhaloka Mawatha, Colombo 7, Sri Lanka
Telephone +94 (11)2504434/5
E-mail ochasrilanka@un.org
Website http://www.un.org.lk

Produced through the generous support of
DFID   Irish Aid   USAID   Canada   Sida

- Map provided courtesy of the UN Office for the Coordination of Humanitarian Affairs
- The boundaries and names shown and the designations used on this map do not imply official endorsement or acceptance by the United Nations

Annex 3

Map 6

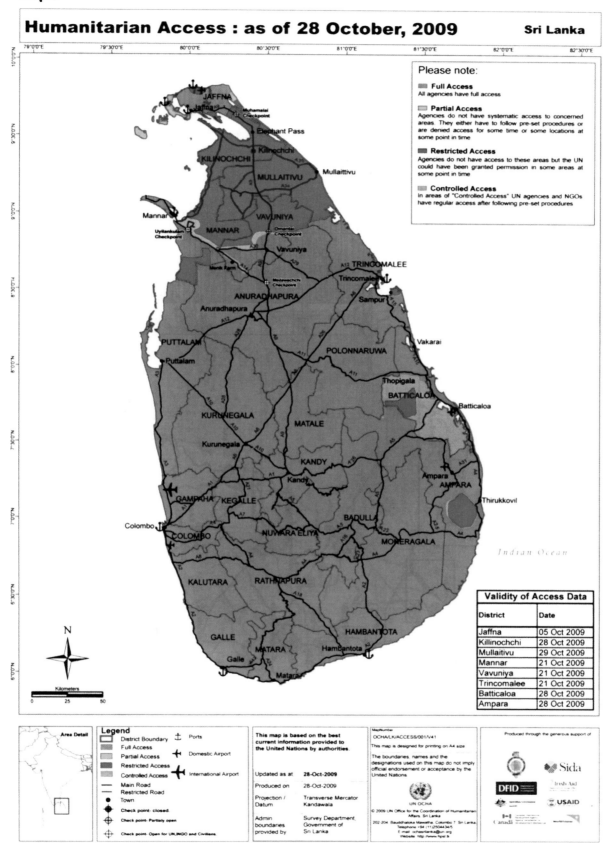

Humanitarian Access : as of 28 October, 2009   Sri Lanka

Please note:

Full Access
All agencies have full access

Partial Access
Agencies do not have systematic access to concerned areas. They either have to follow pre-set procedures or are denied access for some time or some locations at some point in time

Restricted Access
Agencies do not have access to these areas but the UN could have been granted permission in some areas at some point in time

Controlled Access
In areas of "Controlled Access" UN agencies and NGOs have regular access after following pre-set procedures

Validity of Access Data	
District	Date
Jaffna	05 Oct 2009
Killinochchi	28 Oct 2009
Mullaitivu	29 Oct 2009
Mannar	21 Oct 2009
Vavuniya	21 Oct 2009
Trincomalee	21 Oct 2009
Batticaloa	28 Oct 2009
Ampara	28 Oct 2009

Legend
- District Boundary
- Full Access
- Partial Access
- Restricted Access
- Controlled Access
- Main Road
- Restricted Road
- Town
- Check point- closed.
- Check point- Partially open
- Check point- Open for UN,NGO and Civilians.
- Ports
- Domestic Airport
- International Airport

This map is based on the best current information provided to the United Nations by authorities.

Updated as at	28-Oct-2009
Produced on	28-Oct-2009
Projection / Datum	Transverse Mercator Kandawala
Admin boundaries provided by	Survey Department, Government of Sri Lanka

MapNumber
OCHA/LK/ACCESS/001/V41

This map is designed for printing on A4 size

The boundaries, names and the designations used on this map do not imply official endorsement or acceptance by the United Nations

© 2009 UN Office for the Coordination of Humanitarian Affairs, Sri Lanka

Produced through the generous support of

Sida
DFID   Irish Aid
USAID
Canada

- Map provided courtesy of the UN Office for the Coordination of Humanitarian Affairs
- The boundaries and names shown and the designations used on this map do not imply official endorsement or acceptance by the United Nations

Annex 3

Map 7

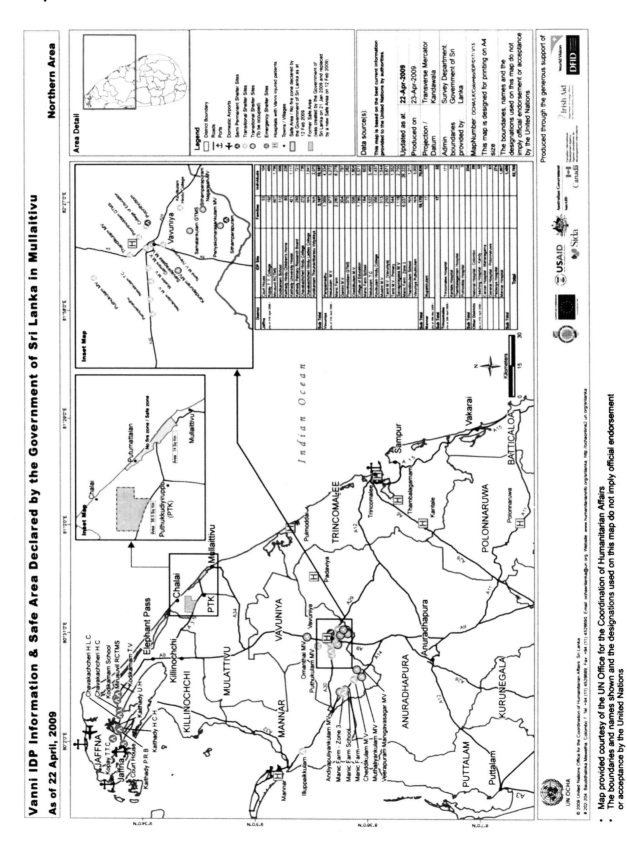

Annex 3

Map 8

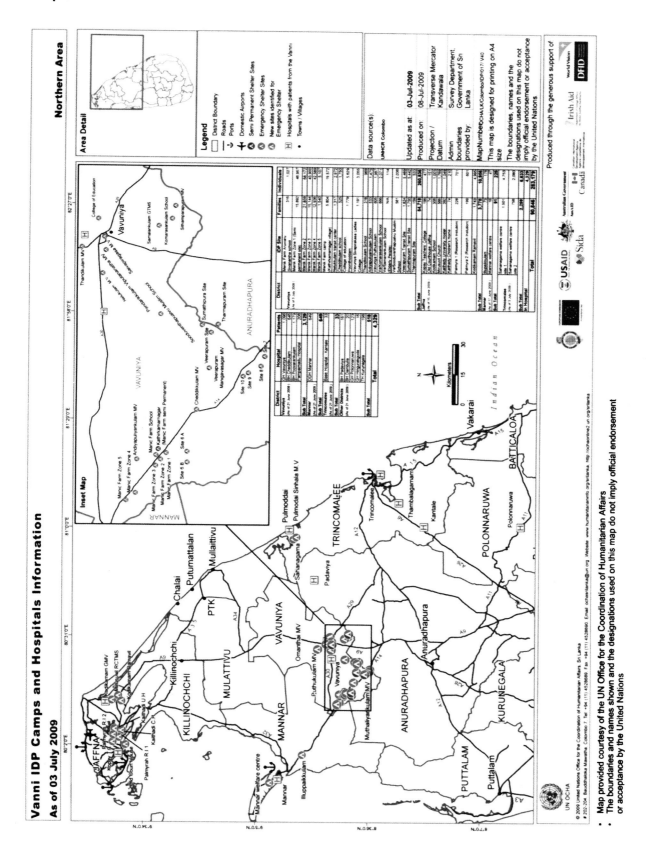

Map 9

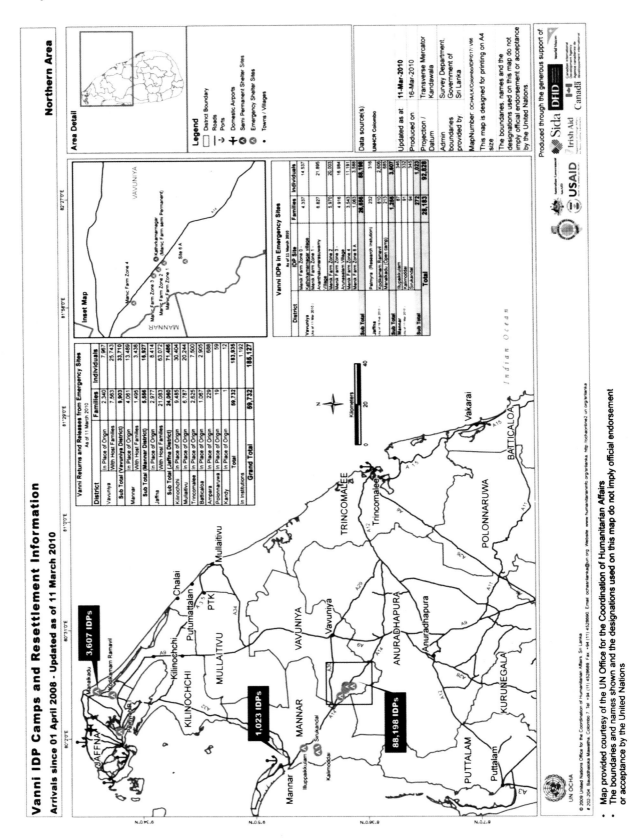

Annex 3

Map 10

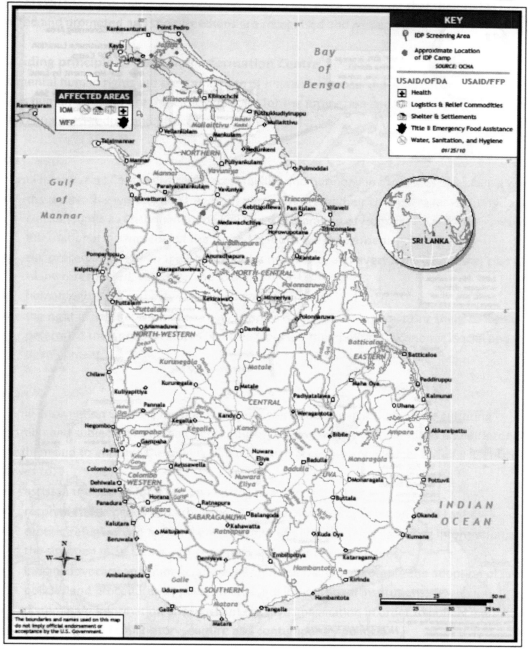

Annex 3

Map 11

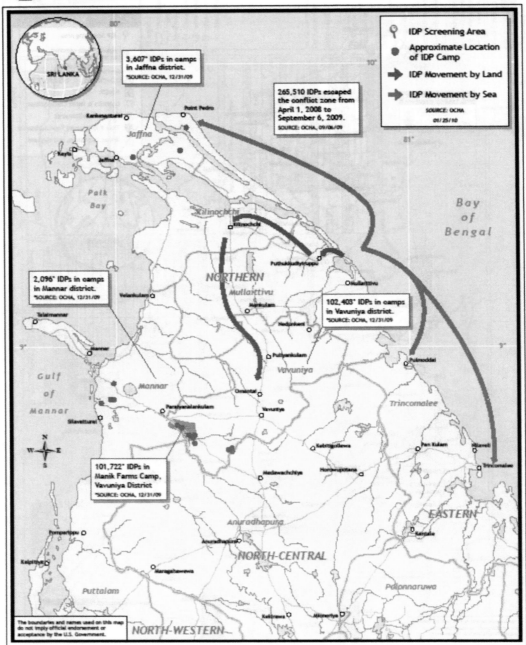

Tamil Information Centre

The Tamil speaking community in Sri Lanka has suffered injustice and oppression for decades and finds it extremely difficult to seek redress in the face of continuing persecution and spurious propaganda and disinformation. The Tamil Information Centre (TIC) endeavours to address the challenges that face the Tamil speaking community in Sri Lanka, to ensure that their rights are protected and promoted and their freedoms are recognised and respected.

The guiding principle of the Tamil Information Centre

Fundamental human rights are the foundation of human existence and co-existence. Human Rights make us human and they are the basic principles for the promotion and achievement of human dignity, equality, freedom and justice.

Vision

The Tamil Information Centre desires peace, stability and harmony in the island of Sri Lanka where:

- the people live with dignity free from persecution and their civil, political, economic and cultural rights as enshrined in the Universal Declaration of Human Rights (UDHR) and other international instruments of the United Nations are recognised;
- self preservation within their homeland is promoted, and every individual in any part of the island is respected, cared for and loved;
- human rights are respected, fostered and promoted;
- the right of self-determination of all peoples is recognised empowering them to freely determine their political status and freely pursue their political, economic, social and cultural development.

Mission

The Tamil Information Centre's mission is to empower people, particularly those suffering persecution and subjected to human rights abuses, valuing the distinct identities and differences among them and to improve the quality of life through access to knowledge. To fulfill its mission the TIC strives to:

- assist in the search for a just and lasting peace in Sri Lanka;
- respond to the needs and problems of victims of war or oppression in Sri Lanka;
- protect refugees and asylum-seekers at risk of persecution by providing information about the situation in Sri Lanka, refugee rights and other relevant issues;
- initiate advocacy and public campaigns on these issues to promote the adoption of just policies and procedures by governments and international institutions;
- disseminate information and works of creative imagination in order to enhance public knowledge on Tamil history, culture and contemporary politics;
- provide facilities for research, consultation, advice and community activities.